The Chipotle Effect

Advance Praise for Author Paul Barron

"Paul is a true visionary. He understands where the restaurant industry is moving in the way that Steve Jobs understood where the personal technology industry was moving. I am in awe of Paul's work and consider him to be a key business and vision mentor."

~ Noah Glass, Founder, OLO.com

"Whenever we need someone to talk about the latest new media technology and social networking techniques in the publishing business we call Paul. He has talked twice at our Niche Magazine Conference and has been outstanding."

~ Carl Landau, CEO, Niche Media

"Paul is an incredible visionary in the communications industry and in the world of branding. While he is grounded in the here and now he can see emerging trends, as evidenced by his early identification of the fast casual segment and the subsequent development of the Fast Casual Alliance. He is uniquely adept at partnering with industry and concept leaders to identify and share these trends."

~ Ed Frechette, Sr. VP, Au Bon Pain

"Working with Paul gave me an honorary MBA in new media. I learned more in my year working with Paul about Web 2.0 and how it interacts with marketing than I could ever learn at any university. His knowledge of new media, and more importantly, how it can be used to market products and services surpasses anything I've learned reading on the Internet."

~ Barry Lauterwasser, Founder, Symbion Marketing

"If I were to compile a list of pioneers for the fast casual industry, Paul Barron would be on it. In The Chipotle Effect, he cements his stature as an astute observer of the industry. He understands the mindset of both the consumer and restaurateur, and combines these insights into a compelling study of the dynamics that have made the fast casual segment the darling of the restaurant industry."

~ Don Fox, CEO, Firehouse Subs

The Chipotle Effect

The changing landscape of the American food consumer
is shifting rapidly, and these changes are having a major impact
on the future of restaurants. Paul Barron, renowned entrepreneur,
publisher, founder of FastCasual.com, and restaurant industry
innovator, explains these changes in this new book.

Paul Barron

Published by Transmedia Press
New York City, NY

CONTENTS

Hot Tip

Follow the hot peppers!

Certain chapters have amazing tips and trends
you won't want to miss.

Chapter One

A Mexican Revolution

You may hate the title of this book, especially if you are involved with a *fast casual* restaurant that is not named Chipotle. It's not especially politically correct of me to name my book after the booming fresh Mexican food chain, but I've always been a person who spoke his mind and pushed the envelope—even while others were getting comfortable and complacent. So this is no different.

The fact is that Chipotle remains shorthand for "remarkable success" in a segment of the restaurant industry that is growing at a dizzying pace, despite the tumultuous economic conditions of the past few years. In 2010, according to a report by Chicago food industry research firm Technomic, the top 100 fast casual chains increased sales 6% in 2010 to $18.9 billion. While that may not seem like a big jump, remember that during the same period most other players in the restaurant world were flat or watching sales crater.

In this book, I will make the case that a large part of that astonishing growth has been due to fast casual's ability to adapt to the changing lifestyles of Americans, including our embrace of social networking and mobile technology. And whether you love them or hate them, no company embodies the strategic embrace and tactical engagement of the new consumer to fuel growth like Chipotle. Heck, in a July 29, 2011 article, FastCasual.com even ran an article titled, "Who will be the Chipotle of the pizza industry?" So even if you don't agree that this Denver-based company is the bellwether of change in our industry, you can't ignore them. So let's look at what Chipotle has done right and how it's changed the restaurant business.

Beginnings

Chipotle may not have fired the first shot in the fast casual revolution, but the fresh Mexican chain is certainly the most famous of the founding fathers. Launched by Steve Ells in a space near the University of Denver in 1993, the restaurant grew quickly, opening its second location in 1995 and continuing its expansion—first with a loan from Ells's father and later with a $1.8 million Small Business Administration loan. Ells, who had no business background, had clearly tapped into an unmet need among diners for healthful, fresh Mexican cuisine, and the Chipotle brand began to take shape: sustainably sourced ingredients, a simple menu, and impeccable quality.

In 1999, Ells opened his first restaurants outside of Colorado, but it was interest from McDonald's Corporation that was the magic bullet for the company's growth. The fast-food titan first approached Ells in 1997 and became a minority investor a year later. Contrary to popular belief, McDonald's did not buy Chipotle but did become its largest investor, sinking more than $360 million into the chain over seven years and helping Chipotle make use of its proven distribution system. By 2005 the chain had more than 500 company-owned restaurants, and in January of 2006 it made its initial public stock offering (IPO), the stock doubling in value on the first day of trading.

In 2006, McDonald's divested itself of its Chipotle holdings, earning about $1.5 billion on its investment. Today, the company has restaurants in 38 states and Canada, was the third-fastest-growing restaurant chain in 2010 according to *Nation's Restaurant News*, and was ranked as the best fast-food Mexican chain in 2011 by

Consumer Reports. Most recently, the company hired award-winning chef Nate Appleman to create new menu items and spearhead the creation of a new fast casual Asian concept restaurant, ShopHouse Southeast Asian Kitchen, which opened in Washington, D.C., in the summer of 2011.

In my humble opinion, Chipotle was simply in the right place at the right time with the right product. But this does not mean that their success has been due to pure luck. You can have the right place, time, and product going for you, but you have to know how to *leverage* them. True, the company was not the first "Fresh Mex" concept, the first burrito player, or the first creative brand builder. But they knew how to grab the gold when the opportunity came. Having watched the mistakes of their predecessors, they were able to develop an in-store and external brand that tapped into what their customers cared about: freshness, quality, sustainability, a sense of humor, and above all, a sense that they were breaking out of the "slightly more upscale fast food" mold of chains like La Salsa and Baja Fresh.

Among other things, Chipotle's success is another nail in the coffin of the "first mover advantage." There have been many companies and people in history who have come late to the dance and yet prevailed as the leader in their industry. It's not always the first mover who winds up "owning" the category; another player who enters the market later and takes advantage of the pioneer's mistakes often rises to the top. Some examples of this are the following:

Nikola Tesla, who, despite his genius, lost out to Thomas Edison in developing the first mass-market electrical utility

Ohioan Elisha Gray, who was working on the telephone at the same time as Scotsman Alexander Graham Bell but got no credit for the invention

New Zealander Richard Pearse, who actually flew a powered aircraft nine months before Orville and Wilbur Wright gained global fame for their flight at Kitty Hawk, North Carolina

Flamboyant pianist Joseph "Jelly Roll" Morton, who may have been the single figure most responsible for creating the music known today as jazz but was completely eclipsed as a pioneer by Duke Ellington and Louis Armstrong.

Want more examples? Here are a few:

* Facebook completely dominates social networking over its predecessor, MySpace.

* Walgreens owns the drugstore market over the much older A&P.

* Sonic has pushed venerable A&W to a niche player.

* Apple's iPhone nearly destroyed the previously dominant Motorola to the point where Motorola's mobile business is now owned by Google.

* Starbucks threatened the survival of the corner coffee shop.

* Barnes & Noble has become the top bookselling brand in the United States while Borders has gone bankrupt.

* Barack Obama was in the right place at the right time with his use of social media to win a presidency.

Don't Pioneer, Perfect

Chipotle has not been the great innovator in the fast casual business. There are several concepts that look better, feel better, and feed consumers better. They did not invent the concept of the fresh food assembly line. They were not the first to introduce sustainably and transparency-sourced ingredients or to apply an industrial design ethos that made the primary colors and hard plastic of the fast-food design palette obsolete. Rarely do pioneers also produce high quality; they are too busy trying to troubleshoot their new ideas to pay attention to fit, finish, and customer experience in order to produce excellence. Apple might be the exception; they managed to both pioneer the definitive online music business model with iTunes while introducing a product that has still not been surpassed. They did the same with the iPhone, defining the smart phone segment.

Chipotle is not the Apple of the restaurant industry. However, their growth has been well nigh unstoppable. There are several reasons for this, the most important of which is that being the first mover in a market space does not automatically confer success. While there is some advantage to be in had being the first player in a market niche (or in creating that niche), doing so more often leaves the first mover quite vulnerable.

Opening your business is, in effect, laying all your cards on the table. (It is possible to be clandestine, but it is rare; few companies are as adept at secrecy as Apple, which has managed to change its industry numerous times while giving its competitors relatively little to work with.) This allows potential competitors to reverse-engineer your company and in doing so build a business model with all of the strengths and none of the weaknesses of the pioneering company. In a sense, early players in a space become de facto testbeds for second-wave entrepreneurs who learn from the errors of their predecessors.

Also, consider the nature of first-wave and second-wave business creators. First movers tend to be pure entrepreneurs—visionaries long on grand ideas and passion and often short on business savvy. Second movers, however, tend to be the opposite. Having watched the first movers and seen the market potential of an idea, they typically approach their emergence into the niche with greater planning, ruthless strategy, and deeper pockets than the first wave. This dynamic often allows second-wave start-ups to benefit from their opponents' mistakes, meet needs that are not being met, and use a given product or service as a launching pad for their own improved or cheaper iteration. In short, being first in a niche is like sticking a target on your back.

Some entrepreneurs have beaten more talented adversaries by simply filing patents first. Others have benefited from the complacency of first movers who thought they could not be toppled or who failed to keep up with the times. Other first-mover companies have done themselves in by failing to exhibit the disciplined thought and action described by Jim Collins in his bestseller *Good to Great*. By creating confusing new menus, launching doomed brand extensions or simply by getting away from what their customers want in an ill-advised pursuit of the new, they left market share on the table for the taking.

By building a credible eco-brand, focusing on a small menu of fresh, top-quality food, and leveraging social media (to name a few of its smart moves), Chipotle has set itself apart from somewhat generic rivals such as Baja Fresh and Wahoo's while taking the best ideas from their older competitors and polishing them into a truly distinctive brand with a hip, high-tech, personal feel that none of the other companies share.

Endangered Species?

Let's set preconceptions about Chipotle's originality or luck aside. For better or worse, the company plays a critical role in the evolution of fast casual. To date, this niche has helped to redefine what dining out is from the ground up. Perhaps the signal change is the decoupling of quality and speed. Prior to the creation of the fast casual segment, the relationship between food quality and speed of service was inverse: the faster you got your food, the lower the quality had to be.

No more. Thanks to Chipotle and other chains that consciously broadcast the quality and freshness of their ingredients, quality and speed are no longer related. On the lowest end of the quality scale remain the traditional fast-food restaurants like Burger King and Taco Bell, where quality remains secondary to speed. But no longer do customers presume that going to a QSR chain like Qdoba or Pei Wei means getting food that's worse than they might get at a traditional casual-dining restaurant. Speed and quality can go together. That perception, which has solidified into fact, has transformed the restaurant industry.

Still, in 25 years we may look back on this as the Golden Age of the restaurant industry. Will this appear to be a period when innovation was abundant and entrepreneurs were bursting at the seams with creativity? Will we view the first dozen years of the twenty-first century as a time when consumer understanding, technology, and lifestyles were calibrated perfectly for the evolution of a new food and service lifestyle for America?

Due to the mammoth successes of chains like Chipotle, Panera, Five Guys, Red Mango,, Firehouse Subs, and Jimmy John's, fast casual is expanding at an amazing rate—one we have to watch closely. Things are changing so quickly that concepts for the next hot Fro-Yo, Better Burger, or Fresh Mex restaurant are becoming irrelevant nearly as quickly as they can be built out. Choice may be at the top of the list for the discerning consumer, but value, quality, experience, and the "Fast Casual X-Factor" are what keep a brand relevant.

"Fast Casual X-Factor is the combination of the perfect product, the perfect experience and the perfect match to the consumer."

This presents a big challenge to today's QSR brands and the new ones breaking in. This includes fast-casual extensions from some of the biggest brands in the restaurant business. Red Robin rolled out Burger Works, its entry into the crowded gourmet burger space, in November 2011. Leveraging its well-known brand, Red Robin will sell a simpler and lower-priced menu of 1/3-pound burgers while also offering beer and wine. Diners will also have a build-your-own-burger option with the choice of beef or chicken patty and a variety of toppings. Burger Works burger will range from $4.49 to $5.99, considerably less than the same burger at the Red Robin parent stores.

IHOP, the granddaddy of Sunday morning sit-down pancake feed restaurants, popped the cork on IHOP Express in San Diego's Gaslamp District after extensive market testing. IHOP Express offers counter service and a limited menu designed for to-go customers. Innovative menu options include the Cup O' Pancakes—served in a cup and topped with strawberry-banana, double blueberry, or caramel apple toppings. Dishes unique to IHOP Express include corncake tacos with meat, shredded cheese and fresh salsa (obviously designed for the Southern California audience), and lower-calorie options from the chain's Simple & Fit menu.

Even fast-food player Wendy's is making a foray into QSR as it tries to remake its brand identity to occupy a space near the higher end of the fast-food firmament. Its first salvo into QSR is the "W" burger, a high-quality burger at a lower price point than most of the major fast-casual burger players. This is a direct play to grab market share from Five Guys and other quality burger builders. Clearly, the established restaurant brands, watching their revenues fall during the recession, are waking up to the potential of fast casual.

Technomic recently stated that the independent restaurant operator could in fact be endangered, and I agree. The fact that celebrity chefs and celebrity restaurateurs are jumping into the multi-unit business, bringing their TV-tested or Michelin-starred brands with them, represents a critical sea change for fast casual. Brands are becoming routine, easily shared, and easily replicated. Consumers get it, too, and for better or worse they are demanding better food and better experiences.

Raising the Stakes

The upscaling of fast casual and the increased expectations of the American consumer have raised the stakes dramatically for all the players and would-be players in this space. The fact is that not all fast-casual chains are organically fast casual; some are watered down versions of bigger players that see the adoption of the systems of fast casual as the key to continued relevance as the market continues to change. The American consumer rightly sees this race to capture his dining dollar as a sign that restaurant operators are willing to bend over backwards to deliver the value and delight that consumers demand—so that consumers are demanding ever more. The result is a punishing race to innovate and re-innovate.

In my opinion, many of the downscaled big players sticking their toes into fast casual will fail in favor of new upscale experiences. Systems, as ground-up fast-casual operators already know, are only part of the package. An organic concept that helps foster a connection with consumers—who feel that the restaurateur "gets" them—is far more important. That's why a new wave of upscale dining ecosystems are already drawing consumers in search of something that works with their self-image and lifestyle. Just a few examples:

* momofuku—This New York-based spinoff of David Chang's sit down restaurants in New York, Toronto, and Sydney is labeled as a "milk bar" and serves an eclectic collection of items from pork buns and pie to, yes, milk. It's willfully eccentric and top quality.

* LYFE Kitchen—This is a major change, a quick-service concept based on health, started by two former McDonald's executives, no less. LYFE is an acronym for "Love Your Food Everyday," and the creators will produce low-calorie, all-natural meals with nothing fried. It's an approach clearly intended to appeal to women and the urban vegan crowd but also a smart angle in an environment where people are more and more concerned about being and staying healthy.

* Vapiano—Style, style, and more style. That's the positioning of this international chain that's specifically targeting young, urban professionals with downtown spaces, dramatic architecture, fresh food, and cocktails. This is fast casual turned upscale hangout. While you might not burn the midnight oil at a location, you might well hit one after a hard day's work, knock back a freshly made salad and a microbrew with friends, and relax for an hour before leaving for another spot. That's precisely what the creators had in mind.

Creations like these are forcing the entire fast-casual world to up its game and become more daring and creative. It's a more merciless environment, and any restaurateurs that can't keep up are likely to be left in the dust.

Chapter Two

From Big Macs to Bread

If fast casual is the latest stage in restaurant evolution, then fast food from In 'N' Out to McDonald's is the ape whose children found a monolith and figured out how to use tools. We can't make sense of the progress of fast casual or the power of the Chipotle Effect without understanding how things began with the fast-food industry and how its transformation field-tested some of the concepts that are turning fast casual into a juggernaut.

We begin, of course, with McDonald's. McDonald's Corporation remains the 800-pound gorilla in the QSR category and the titan of fast food. Name an advance in QSR operations—drive-thru service, numbered value meals, playgrounds that turn restaurants into family-friendly destinations—and McDonald's probably pioneered or perfected it. Richard and Maurice McDonald opened the first location in San Bernardino, California, in 1940 and quickly created many of the speedy-service conventions so widely used in fast food today.

However, the modern titan was born in 1955 when Ray Kroc opened a franchised restaurant in Des Plaines, Illinois. Kroc bought out the McDonald brothers' equity share in the chain (possibly the worst investment decision in history) and aggressively expanded the company's footprint nationally and internationally. Today, McDonald's serves approximately 64 million customers a day in about 31,000 restaurants scattered throughout 119 countries. In 2010, McDonald's Corporation earned an operating income of $7.473 billion on total revenues of $24 billion.

This growth has not come without a price, however. McDonald's has come to be viewed around the world as the harbinger of "creeping Americanization," the spread of tacky, soulless, manufactured American culture. This has produced an anti-McDonald's backlash in countries such as France. Concerns over the health impact of the company's food, fanned by films such as *Super Size Me!* and books such as *Fast Food Nation*, have also forced McDonald's to revamp its menu to include healthier choices. More recently, the chain has also begun redesigning its restaurants to be more in line with the more upscale feel commonly found in fast-casual dining. Disappearing are the stark white, yellow, and red "clown colors" hard-edged plastic and swiveling chairs. Décor more akin to Starbucks—café tables, armchairs, softer lighting, and a more adult atmosphere—represents McDonald's transition into the post-fast-food age.

In a way, the anti-McDonald's sentiment around the world may have been one of the factors behind the rise of fast casual. Eager to distance themselves from the tacky, florid, "ugly American" image attached to the Golden Arches, chains like Panera and Chipotle have from the start embraced healthier menu items, restrained design palettes, and hipper, tech-friendly amenities such as online ordering and free WiFi. Ronald McDonald may in fact be the forefather of Noodles & Company and Corner Bakery.

Changing Reluctantly

In the mid 1990s, while starting FastCasual.com, I had to pay the bills, so I took a few consulting gigs in retail system design and worked with McDonald's in their innovation center in Romeoville, Illinois. It's quite a place: a full functioning McDonald's hidden inside a large complex that looked much like an industrial plant. Inside this center, the QSR equivalent of mad scientists test-drove all sorts of innovations in the customer experience: kiosks, remote ordering, even the McCafe.

Yes, the McCafe. The Starbucks-esque premium coffee brand that has helped to revitalize the Golden Arches began in the 1990s. At the same time, the company was experimenting with split-lane drive-thru. The consumer was beginning to demand a new, more sophisticated style from its eating establishments, and even McDonald's, long recognized as the ultimate family restaurant, was not immune to the trend. However, the company was not enthusi-astic about adapting to the times. I won't mention names, but my ideas for transitioning the brand to that of a more upscale, fast casual-style operation were not well received. The pushback was forceful; the commitment to selling Big Macs absolute, even if that wasn't what the market was asking for. I even heard statements like, "We are not a foo-foo coffee house, we sell Big Macs and fries!"

That said, perhaps in spite of the overall anti-change corporate attitude, a variety of new menu items—including the McCafe and fresh salads—developed during this period. These items, which were far outside the traditional McDonald's menu, brought the deeply conservative chain closer to fast-casual territory. However, by 1999 the project was dead. McDonald's would spend another half decade trying to force its high-calorie menu items down the world's throats

until greater public awareness of nutrition and a demand for healthier menu choices forced it to resurrect much of the work that we did
in the 1990s. So, happily, the all-nighters we pulled trying to fine-
tune the food and the service were not wasted.

At the time, McDonald's could not accept that fast casual would
both change America and the company's place as the quintessential
American food brand. Like most hugely successful companies, they
were plagued with a certain degree of complacency. However, they
did finally embrace change and support the evolution of their brand.
Overall, McDonald's successfully turned a business the size of the
British ship *Queen Elizabeth II*—until it headed in a new direction—
away from the icebergs of irrelevance, if I may push the metaphor
a bit. The most visible changes the company undertook also set the
stage for another high-flying fast-casual brand.

A Lot of Bread

If you walk into a Panera location (and there are a lot of them)
and squint, it's easy to imagine that you're at a McDonald's from a
few years back. There's the counter with the menu board, the bright
colors, the family atmosphere. Then when you open your eyes, you
see the differences: muted lighting, more pleasing surfaces and
materials, and of course, a far different menu. But make no mis-

take, a lot of the credit for the attractive, "sticky" quality of Panera and similar fast-casual chains goes to McDonald's, which first made them acceptable.

However, Panera's management did the rest. This is a brand that took the simple bakery business to new heights. How could a simple staple like bread be improved upon? That's the beauty of fast casual: because the consumer has come to expect a more sensory, pleasurable experience from brands in this space, it is easier to take something simple and make it elegant and memorable. The best brands in the marketplace do more than deliver food. They create experiences and environments where customers want to spend time.

When you walk into Panera, the aroma of baking bread and the immediate rush of warmth hit you square in the senses. The low light and classy color scheme don't scream at you. Instead, they invite you in. The well-placed bakery case, the smell of the coffee, the allure of the community-style seating—these factors and others seems to bring in businesspeople and students in droves. In fact, walk into a Panera in an urban area and you'll probably see an ocean of students on their laptops, pecking away and tapping into the restaurant's wireless Internet. In a fast-food joint, they would probably be asked to leave as soon as they finished their meals. Not here. In the fast-casual model, the goal is as much to craft a mental space where people want to hang out as much as it is to sell lots of food. Panera is part of the new ethos: restaurant as community gathering spot.

Panera Bread began taking shape back in 1993 when the chain Au Bon Pain bought the St. Louis Bread Company, established in 1981. In 1999, the company sold its Au Bon Pain restaurant chain to Compass Group North America and renamed itself Panera Bread. Since that time, the business has grown to 1,453 company-owned or franchised stores in 40 states and Canada, with total 2010 revenues of $1.54 billion and profits of $111.9 million. *Health* magazine called Panera the healthiest fast-casual restaurant in North America, and it has received many other accolades for healthy options and its welcoming environment.

Are You Enchanted Yet?

Hot Tip

But how? How has Panera worked its magic when plenty of other bread and baked goods stores have come up short? People often ask me, "Can fast casual be replicated in other business models that have service as their primary product?" My answer? Absolutely. Food is not the killer app. Other companies make better bread than Panera. What sets Panera's leadership apart is an understanding of how consumers connect to the simplicity of food and relate it to their overall experience. That is the real key to breaking down all kinds of retail and service walls in the future.

Let's get crazy for a few minutes. Let's port the fast-casual model into an industry with which it has nothing obvious in common: healthcare. The harsh reality of an aging population, the near-universal unpleasantness of the typical health care experience and the growing need of consumers wanting to feel special goes against the grain of the typical doctor's office. What will you find there? Most likely a dated lobby stocked with outdated magazines, furnished with hideously uncomfortable tubular steel chairs and generic lithographs, and staff who barely acknowledge your presence. It's not exactly a warm, welcoming place to enter when you've been fasting or are nursing a sprained ankle.

So let's transform this office according to the dictates of fast casual. First, we consider what happens before you even get to the door. Is the brand message alluring, comforting, and personal, suggesting a holistic experience and a doctor who listens? Do the exterior colors and signage support that impression? Now, is a glass door with a bunch of MD names stenciled on it the way to make patients feel welcome? No. The message is, "It's all about us." An entrance with graphics showing families and healthy lifestyles tells prospective patients that you, the physician, are here for them instead of the other way around.

Enter the lobby. The seating arrangement looks like something from a hip urban loft. The lighting is low, the décor clean and inviting. From the traffic flow and the method of signing in (preferably a tablet computer or touch screen) to the entertainment and the staff training, everything can be improved, turning what was a depersonalizing or even frightening experience to one that is pleasant, educational, and life-affirming. Patients not only feel connected to the clinic but become evangelists because you conveyed a simple message: "We are all about *you*."

Now let's take a trip over to the Starbucks after that morning physical in the sterile, stale doctor's office. What a difference! The aromas, the furnishings, the colors, the sonic textures, the signage—everything contributes to the Message: *This is your place.* Starbucks has positioned itself as that special place where you can meet a friend, read a book, get caught up on email, get to know your new iPad, log into free wireless Internet, or even buy a cup of coffee. The customer education, the creativity, the content, and the culture all have a specific meaning and goal. They say to the customer, "We are not just here to sell you coffee, snacks, CDs, or espresso makers. We want to enhance your life."

That is what Guy Kawasaki calls *enchantment*, and it's fundamental to the success of fast casual. All thriving chains enchant their customers in some way. Enchantment, according to the original Apple evangelist and all-around master of buzz and creating customer delight, is an elusive quality that could be best described as using trust, authenticity, a good cause, simplicity, great names and titles, and consistent personal connection to turn perfect strangers into enthusiastic, cheerleading fans of you or your company. In his latest book, also called *Enchantment*, Kawasaki says that it's more than branding, which can be seen (and often is) manipulative.

Extremely successful boutique businesses do this all the time. Knowing they cannot compete with big-box stores on price or product selection, they instead create unique, tactile, highly personal experiences for their customers with packaging, direct mail, personal shoppers, and innumerable other small touches that add up to enormous loyalty and even love.

The design, personnel, and atmosphere of the successful fast-casual establishment (like Starbucks) invite, soothe, and give the guest permission to project himself or herself on the space. *This place is about you, not us*, the enchanting environment says. When you walk into a Starbucks, especially since the company has been renovating many of its stores to fit local architecture, you get a sense of sophistication, material comfort, and peace. You can talk, work on your laptop, take business calls, or—heaven forbid—just drink a cup of espresso at your own pace.

Get in line at Chipotle and you don't feel herded like a sheep, as some early critics described the company's line-up-to-order strategy. Because the servers are friendly and fast, you feel catered to, your food custom-made. The interior, all clean lines and corrugated metal, lends an air of urban chic, and the clever messaging about the company's sustainable practices seems transparent and fun.

Enchantment manages to walk the finest of lines: calculated, strategic outreach to customers that manages not to *appear* calculated or strategic because it is backed by authentic values, a passion for an honest exchange with the customer, and the desire to do good. It's long been observed that U.S. consumers are both cynical and smart; enchantment can only work if it's from the heart.

Chapter Three

The Third Place

"Customers don't always know what they want. The decline in coffee drinking was due to the fact that most of the coffee people bought was stale and they weren't enjoying it. Once they tasted ours and experienced what we call 'the third place,' a gathering place between home and work where they were treated with respect... they found we were filling a need they didn't know they had."

— *Howard Schultz*

In the 1990s, consumer savvy and creativity were at all-time highs as technology and an increased awareness of the methods of mass marketing made for consumers ready to drive demand and not just be driven to purchase products and services. Restaurant industry thinkers began to apply the famous Moore's Law (the high-tech maxim that states that microprocessing power doubles every eighteen months) to the fast-casual segment, implying that the number of total restaurant locations would double at approximately the same rate. But that was not to be the case.

In the mid 1990s, the emergence of AOL and the World Wide Web enabled millions of people to share information and discover new worlds instantly. Search engines, beginning with Yahoo!, Lycos, and Alta Vista, changed how we looked for facts and organized the world. Information junkies were born, and as people became more informed they became more skeptical—even cynical—about marketing. The pompous, manipulative tactics of the QSR industry's past seemed not only quaint but ineffective and actually counterproductive.

The country's lifestyle began to shift to a much more aware consumer, one who demanded transparency and authenticity. This "new consumer," empowered by email and other tools, would penalize companies that did not deliver value or respond to customer communications.

Not Home, Not Work

Into this environment came Starbucks and one of the most
brilliant concepts in the history of fast casual: the "third place." The
now-ever-present coffee chain began with a single store selling coffee beans and roasting supplies, which opened on Western Avenue
in Seattle in 1971 (the location moved in 1975 to the famous Pike
Place Market, where it remains today). After the founders sold
the company to former Director of Marketing Howard Schultz's Il
Giornale chain in 1987, the Starbucks brand exploded.

Schultz had always been a proponent of selling espresso and
gourmet coffee in his restaurants, something the Starbucks founders had opposed. With the inclusion of ever more exotic types of
beans in the stores, paired with Schultz's aggressive expansion poli-
cies, Starbucks went global. The company filed its IPO in 1992 and
quickly became so ubiquitous that it became the subject of parody
on such TV programs as *The Simpsons*, which lampooned the ten-
dency for new Starbucks stores to pop up on the same block, across
the street from one another, in such cities as New York and Boston.

Whatever the cultural snickering, by the end of 2010, Starbucks
had its own entertainment label, a branded food division, more than
17,000 stores worldwide, and $10.7 billion in revenues.

Of course, with this growth and success came a backlash. Schultz, who had stepped down as CEO in 2000, returned in 2008 to restore what he saw as the company's small-company culture after sales fell in the face of too-rapid expansion and dilution of the brand. The quality of Starbucks coffee was widely derided and their cookie-cutter stores were the subjects of successful protests in character-sensitive towns such as Ocean Beach, California.

Under Schultz, the company has closed locations, redesigned stores to be in line with local architecture, brought in premium brewing equipment and emphasized fair trade and environmental programs. Fatefully, Schultz also introduced the concept of the "third place." His idea was that while consumers had home as their "first place" and work as their "second place," people lacked a neutral location that was neither home nor work where they could gather, spend time, and perhaps partake of good food and beverages. Possibly inspired by the European concept of the salon, Schultz began to promote Starbucks locations as that in-between locale.

There, so the reasoning went, consumers could relax in comfortable surroundings marked by a sophisticated design ethos, chat with friends or co-workers, use free wireless Internet to hatch plans for start-up companies, work on their screenplays or whatever their hearts desired, all while gourmet coffee drinks and tidbits were available an arm's length away. Crucially, baristas were trained never to pressure customers to buy any products, which is why today you can walk into a Starbucks, work for hours, use the bathrooms and WiFi, and never be hassled to purchase a venti latte or a short-bread cookie. Because of this genius positioning and the welcoming customer experience that resulted, Starbucks has indeed become the "third place" in the lives of millions. In a very real sense, it has become the new McDonald's—the restaurant where you can always count on a clean bathroom, friendly service and quality products, no matter where in the world you are.

While the company has been accused of everything from "gre-enwashing" and "local-washing" to wiping out the mom-and-pop java huts in small towns from coast to coast, the many savvy moves orchestrated by Schultz and his compatriots have redeemed the Starbucks image to a great degree, and the company's position as the third place seems quite secure.

The only threat to that standing might be Panera, the other fast-casual powerhouse that has done the most to turn its restaurants into laid-back hangouts where customers feel comfortable kick-ing back working on their laptops for hours, and of course, buying more food. Panera is now thought to be the biggest purveyor of free WiFi in the country, attracting a customer demographic—college students and young entrepreneurs—that would make a television advertising executive's iPad screen fog over with envy.

Of course, that was until Starbucks started offering free WiFi at all its locations—a perfect example of how competitive pressures can yield tremendous benefits for consumers, as well as unexpected impacts for business. Today, if you walk into a Panera location in an urban area, you'll probably see signs asking customers to limit their stays during peak hours so as not to monopolize the available broadband access and seating. Starbucks may face the same pressures, but if it does you wouldn't know it: baristas never pressure customers to buy product in order to use WiFi. In any case, the desire to appeal to the all-powerful consumer is compelling even the biggest players to roll out attractive new features whenever possible.

True, a majority of fast-casual players will probably never aspire to turn their stores into "third place" style hangouts, because their business models are simply not built on that kind of cache or "sticky" quality. Even so, the uniqueness of having major chain restaurants creating inviting, holistic experiences for the customer (rather than "turning and burning" every available table with high-pressure sales tactics) has utterly transformed consumer expectations for the segment.

Revitalizing an American Classic

Did Starbuck's plan its assault on the U.S. market in hopes of owning the concept of the third place and stoking demand for a new culinary and beverage experience, or was it the perfect storm of technology, consumer savvy, and the desire for a different experience? The jury is still out. What I do know is that along with giving birth to the third place meme, the coffee giant also led the revivification of an American icon, the drive-thru window.

To be sure, they didn't invent it. Several restaurant companies claim to have had the first drive-up food service, including In-N-Out Burger (which claims it launched the idea in 1948 at their restaurant in Baldwin Park, California) and Jack-in-the-Box in 1951. Whatever its origins, drive-thru service became as American as apple pie, a symbol of the burgeoning car culture of the 1950s and 1960s.

The strategic placement of drive-thrus along the newly built interstate highway system quickly put convenience—along with the element of cool and hip—as close as the next highway exit. It let middle-class Americans experience a quasi-futuristic new phenomenon while also democratizing the idea of affordable service on the go.

Starbucks quickly made its mark in this classic niche of American food and beverage consumption. The company started testing the market for drive-up lattes in—where else—auto-dominated Southern California back in 1994. By this time, drive-thrus had been around so long that they had become expected, then passé. There was nothing sexy about them. However, no one had tried to service the country's growing caffeine addiction via the drive-thru lane, either. Starbucks management surmised that busy commuters would flock to an already-trusted quick service brand for their morning Joe if they could get their fix without leaving their vehicles.

Score another win for the mermaid.

I'm often asked, "Can you get great quality from a drive-thru window?" After all, the speed and portability needed to shovel food and drinks at drivers at high speed would seem to be counter to the idea of good taste. At one point that was my position, but it's changed. Technology has caught up with drive-thru culture. Not only have ordering systems increased customer throughput, but more advanced equipment has made it possible for restaurants to keep up with faster ordering and speedier food preparation. The result? Food can be made fresh rather than reheated in the time it takes for a customer to order, drive to a pay window, pay, and drive to the pickup window, all with a minimal wait.

So today, I would answer yes, it is possible to get quality food and beverages via a drive-thru window, provided the company in question has made quality—not speed—the main selling point of its brand. As consumers demand greater and greater efficiency to keep pace with their busy lives, drive-thru will actually become more important, and new paradigms within that segment will no doubt elevate quality to a point undreamt-of by the creators of the first fast-food drive-thrus.

In the end, the growing mobile culture—mobile phones were just beginning to shrink and become truly affordable—made the drive-thru experiment a rousing success. By 2001, Starbucks had 170 drive-thru coffeehouses in operation; by 2005 it had more than 1,000. Today, according to *USA Today*, nearly one-third of the approximately 11,000 U.S. Starbucks locations have drive-thru lanes. It's hard to imagine a better match: the dominant coffee brand gone mobile, matched with the incredible growth in mobile technology symbolized by the dominant brand in mobile technology, Apple and its iPhone and iPad. And with that segue...

Chapter Four

Yelps, Tweets, and iPhones, Oh My!

The incredible rise in the popularity and power of mobile communications and computing technology has both fueled and directed the growth in the fast-casual segment. Since the two-pound "brick" phones of the late 1980s, mobile phone technology had blossomed from a luxury to a necessity, and prices had come down. The tech and the lifestyle it powered were perfectly aligned to spark a new era in casual dining in which the consumer wanted his or her food to be as quick and mobile as he or she was.

The smart phone is an order of magnitude more powerful and versatile than its precursors. The first commercially available mobile phone, the DynaTAC 8000x, came out in 1983, weighed more than 1.5 pounds and had a one-hour battery life. Despite these limitations, companies from all over the world quickly jumped into the market and advanced the technology. The first 2G network launched in 1991 in Finland; the first 3G network began taking calls in 2001 in Japan, courtesy of NTT DoCoMo.

Growth of mobile phone usage has been exponential. In impoverished countries, where infrastructure is poor or nonexistent, mobile phones have become essential tools. Overall, in 2001 there were approximately one billion mobile phone subscribers world-wide, the same number as land line users. Today, according to the International Telecommunication Union, there are more than 5.3 billion subscribers, led by China, which has more than 860 million mobile users. This technology has placed us in an entirely new ter-ritory in the retail and restaurant business. It's steeper and more dangerous, but for those who can manage the climb and plan to overcome the sheer drops, it will be more rewarding. Mobile technol-ogy and the data cloud are utterly transforming the landscape with regard to consumer interaction, customer engagement, and the abil-ity of people to shift the emphasis of businesses from us to them. If you're in the restaurant industry, it's no longer all about you; it's about how you can make your establishment relate to the custom-er's wants, needs, and constantly shifting self-assigned identity.

Mobile computing and the web of social networks have shifted the balance of power. Anyone who wants to be relevant in five years must have a digital business strategy that encompasses not only smart phones, tablet computing, and social networking but also personalized advertising, digital currency, remote ordering, and the desire for 24/7 gaming and entertainment as part of the dining experience. The clock never stops running, and the empowered New Consumer is timing everybody to see who will dazzle and delight him next. While technological prowess cannot and should not push out quality food and excellent service as barometers of performance, the purveyors who can find ways to deliver both with greater high-tech convenience, speed, and panache will dominate in the next decade.

The iPhone Cometh

The mobile computing platform began its climb to world domination with the 2004 release of the iPhone and later with the development of the Android operating system, now the most popular mobile OS in the world. These innovations took the mobile phone out of the realm of a pure communications device and made it into the first truly portable computing platform—and the fact that this platform was connected 24/7 to a national (or global) datastream via cell towers and satellites magnified its potential exponentially. In the space of a few years, millions of consumers had become mobile media studios, reporters, and opinion shapers.

The mobile phone's evolution from a handheld communications device to a mobile computing platform completed the handover of segment-shaping power in the restaurant industry from reviewers and traditional media to the consumer. The transition began with the Internet and sites like Yelp and Trip Advisor, but prior to the advent of the powerful mobile computer, the stationary nature of the Internet meant that diners either could not easily access online restaurant information and reviews or lost their motivation to post it by the time they returned home.

Smart phones started the shift away from passive to active participation in the restaurant information ecosystem. That shift has reached tectonic levels due to the market-shaping popularity of tablet computing personified by Apple's iPad. Now, individuals who previously used their iPhones or other smart phones to locate restaurants and share their opinions about them via Twitter, but who might have been put off typing long reviews by the small phone keypads, had a new platform.

As tablets replace laptops in the lives of millions (as of June 2011 Apple was estimated to have sold 25 million iPads), consumers have become even more empowered to tweet, update, and post reviews about the dining establishments that please and displease them. This activity has forced even Luddite restaurant operators to "tech up" with new websites, presences on Facebook and so on. For tech-savvy companies like Chipotle (which, for example, maintains an active Facebook page with more than 1.5 million fans), the demands of "power users" of mobile tools has become a gold mine of opportunities for outreach and personal contact.

A Two-Way Relationship

The number of power users who rely almost exclusively on mobile computing for their computing needs is booming. Apple has sold more than 60 million iPhones worldwide, while Google's free Android OS is experiencing year-on-year growth of more than 800% across 60 devices in over 40 countries. Smart phones have tipped the balance of information in the consumer's favor, allowing users to use Twitter, GPS data, and review websites to find restaurants with the characteristics and reviews that suit them and to post their own opinions in real time.

More and more, any restaurant chain that does not have both social media and mobile media strategies is working from a severe competitive disadvantage. On the other hand, operators who know how to leverage the platform can use it to power growth. One example is the now-famous Kogi Korean BBQ truck. Beginning in 2009, the operators of the single Korean-Mexican fusion mobile diner got the idea to begin promoting their food via Los Angeles bloggers and then on Twitter. As word got out about the quality of Kogi's food, they began advertising the location of their truck exclusively by tweet, ensuring extensive retweeting. As a result of this social buzz, hundreds of hungry Angelinos would often show up at the truck's location even in the wee hours of the morning. Today, Kogi has five L.A.-area trucks and has just opened its first sit-down establishment, but more importantly, they launched the Food Truck phenomenon now booming in cities like Washington, DC, Miami, Chicago, Austin, and New York.

Much as fast casual completely upended the public's perception of what quickly produced food could be (better than rewarmed fastfood and cheaper than a sit-down café), the Food Truck movement has taken what were once seen as mobile greasy spoons and turned them into "street cuisine" with high levels of authenticity and local flair. More and more cities—from Springfield, Illinois, to Alameda, California—are clearing the regulatory paths for mobile dining, providing consumers with yet another means to get fantastic, fresh food on a budget—while mingling with a local crowd.

We have entered the era of the two-way fast-casual relationship. No longer can restaurateurs assume that the one-direction dynamic of "we make the food, you eat the food" is acceptable to consumers. This is an interactive business now. The new era of mobile technology has emerged as the most intimate means for consumers to experience restaurants and retailers of all types. By using the myriad available tools wisely and actively, companies can connect with their customers and develop word-of-mouth relationships in ways that would have taken weeks or even months in the old world.

In this new dynamic, local is everything. Tapping into location-based media is the long-sought Holy Grail of the restaurant industry. Google has taken its shot with Google Places, its local business search engine. Social media plays a major role in this as well. But the real question is this: "With all the noise, how do I break away from the pack in my own market?"

Foursquare has provided one path to this. With their fast, furious adoption of location-based services (LBS) like Foursquare, consumers have shown by their actions that they are willing to divulge their whereabouts in return for learning more about local businesses. Foursquare launched in 2009, created by Dennis Crowley and Naveen Selvadurai as a location-based social network for mobile devices such as smartphones. Users "check-in" at venues they frequent such as bars and restaurants using either a text message, website, or mobile app. The more often a user frequents a location, the greater his or her status within the network.

Users can leave "messages" on the network about certain locations and find their friends in geographic space, making Foursquare a powerful tool for real-time dining decisions. Due in great part to this relatively seamless integration with "meatspace," the company in 2011 passed seven million registered users and has a valuation of about $600 million. It's likely that Foursquare will shift their model soon and transition the value of mapping most of the global restaurant map and where people go with a more Yelp-like system. I also expect consolidation in LBS to the big three in Facebook, Twitter, and Google in the future.

This kind of tightly integrated, highly practical, local social networking and contact with consumers is on the path to a new kind of popularity. I foresee in the near future that the ways that local networks will most benefit restaurateurs will not be the traditional advertising channels but mini food networks that focus on what's the best of what's around us. For example, Gilt City is Groupon based on luxury. Lockhart Steele may be local's great visionary with his empire of food, fashion, design, and real estate: Eater.com, Racked.com, and Curbed.com. Thinkers like Steele are transforming how we think of local—taking it hyper-local. Consumers know what they know, and they know what's in their towns and neighborhoods. These new apps, social networks, and technology platforms respect and empower that knowledge.

Local Influencers

Hot Tip

This has given rise to a new subset of technology power player: the local influencer. Certainly, there are still influencers whose ideas and comments dictate how brands act on a global level, but the local influencer may be the trump card everyone has been seeking. Growing any business requires you to connect at the local level. It requires community involvement, connecting with the dominant local personalities, and understanding how to reach them in the digital spaces where they live.

By mid 2012, I will have more than 100,000 Twitter followers. That gets me plenty of attention, but my most satisfying times come when I engage with a local business—no matter where I am. Multiply that by 100 when the engagement is in my backyard. Engaged local businesses understand where I am checking in from, where I go on Friday nights, and maybe even what wine I drink or what beach I like. They know me, and my opinions mean something to them. That matters. That is currency. This currency is a new way for restaurant operators to look into the minds of consumers and build brands. This is the new mantra every small business—especially restaurants—should adopt:

Going local is a wonderful way to overcome the online and mobile overload that many consumers and business owners are experiencing. As Ryan Spoon pointed out on BusinessInsider.com, local merchants face an overload of tech "must connects," from Google to Yelp to Facebook. An intense local focus cuts through that and allows for greater authenticity and impact. When we begin to analyze how our local markets interact with us, the data silos that reside in places like Twitter, Facebook, Foursquare, and Google Plus will be the deal killer for every traditional advertising model out there. Soon, a generation will be born that will have no idea what Yellow Pages are.

How does this tie into fast casual, specifically? Well, most fast-casual brands are extremely local. At best, they are regional with the potential to break out, if they get very lucky, to a global market. But while Starbucks has left Seattle far behind and Chipotle is no longer confined to Denver, most fast-casual chains will remain regional affairs. The thing is that with the hyper-local networks building today, this is a strength, not a weakness. The smart business operator understands that to excel in the global economy is to do one thing really well. For many fast-casual operators, that means dominating their local and regional markets. Local is a vibrant, consumer-driven, socially charged storm that cannot be calmed and will keep evolving, making it hard for fast-casual executives to keep up. Those that do will be rewarded with market share.

46%

of consumers are now using mobile devices
to access information on restaurants

You Must Be Mobile

The impact of this hyper-local focus, powerful handheld computing technology, and the mobile, interactive lifestyle is multiplied by the onslaught of mobile apps being downloaded by consumers onto phones and tablets. Apps like UrbanSpoon, Zagat, and Trip Advisor enable users to find and review restaurants all over the country. Apps like Open Table empower mobile reservations, while apps like VeganXpress let consumers search for specific types of cuisine. Apps are enhancing browser-based applications as the power platform of choice for consumers who have come to feel entitled to share and know the consensus opinion on virtually any dining establishment—and who are more than willing to base their dining decisions on such "crowdsourced" restaurant intelligence resources like Foodspotting, Pinterest and Oink (the rating app created by Digg founder Kevin Rose).

As the smart phone replaces the computer as a platform for interaction, search and social contact, every fast-casual operator must develop or refine a mobile development strategy. This strategy will respond to consumer reviews, create multiple points of personal connection, and create convenience and transparency that would have been unthinkable a generation ago. Mobile social media has already become a mainstay in any organization looking to reach today's consumer.

The good news is that the fast-casual operator is already perfectly positioned to make mobile and social media an organic component of his or her business model. After all, some of the defining characteristics of a successful fast-casual operation are personal connection with customers, speed of service, compelling design, and transparency of operations, such as where ingredients are sourced. These qualities dovetail beautifully with the dominant mobile and social cultures, which value instant delivery of value, authenticity, and quality design. Add a tech-smart element and it's easy to see that social media, mobile computing, and fast casual were made for each other.

Mobile + Social + Local

Mobile will continue to drive consumer interaction and the geo-metric growth of word of mouth (or perhaps word of touchscreen) marketing at a startling pace; I expect it to double or triple in the next 24 months. Any fast-casual business not engaged in Location Based Services, or LBS (in which consumers use mobile GPS to access information or entertainment content provided by the business), or some other sort of compelling mobile interaction, will face huge competitive pressures.

Expect the evolution of new app and mobile technologies driven by restaurant operators, new marketing and public relations strategies linked to social media, and organizational shifts as companies develop internal disciplines and divisions to control and optimize their social and mobile interactions. As the world forces it to change, fast casual is pushing forward as a change agent all its own.

Hot Tip

What's Possible

Speaking of change agents, if you don't believe that technology can

change the world on a dime, take a look at these examples of disruptive

tech evolution:

* Mashable and Peter Cashmore—Pete Cashmore launched Mashable from his home in Aberdeen, Scotland, in 2005. Today, the social media and entertainment news site is one of the world's most popular Web destinations, with more than 50 million monthly page views.

* TechCrunch and Mike Arrington—Arrington also launched his technology news website in 2005, and it quickly grew into a monster network with more than 4.5 million RSS subscribers. In 2010, AOL bought TechCrunch for $25 million.

* TWiT Network and Leo Laporte—Now TWiT.tv, this rising star began in 2005 (what is it about that year?) as a podcast and now hosts multiple podcasts and streaming shows covering subjects like the Internet, Apple, computer security and Microsoft. Today, TWiT.tv has a new, state-of-the-art studio in Petaluma, California, and gross revenues approaching $3 million annually.

* Revision3—Revision3 is a fast-growing Internet television network that specializes in niche topics. Founded in—you guessed it—2005, the network has become an important hub of edgy content that appeals to tightly focused audiences and is perfect for local marketing and communication.

* Eater.com—The previously mentioned Eater.com has become a force in the restaurant industry and among food elites, providing clever, edgy coverage of restaurants, chefs, and the restaurant business from coast to coast.

* Funny, I merged FastCasual.com with my media partners in 2005 and began the Fast Casual Alliance and the Fast Casual Summit in 2005. The connection to tech and how consumers were connecting is road-mapped nicely to the expansion of fast casual.

At this writing I find myself in a new era of identifying a whole new arena of disruptive companies and leaders that will remap the restaurant and retail business of the future—and it's not the guys you think. Technology, the Web, and the creative innovation of a whole new generation is upon us, and the era of the good-old-boys network is on its way out for the soon-to-be $800 billion industry. Think "Restaurant Disrupt" and you will get the picture really fast. Everything is in a shift, new galaxies are being created as we speak in this space, and the typical team of operators and innovators are leading us to a new business model for the future.

The point is that all these media companies and even the consumer platforms and others like them did not exist just a few years ago. In five to six years they have redefined the *entire* information, entertainment, and consumer behavior landscape. In perhaps ten percent of the time that television grew to become a dominating cultural force, the Internet, mobile media, and social networks have risen to eclipse the traditional broadcast and print media that spawned them. Everything is possible, and everything is faster. This creates new opportunities for fast casual—provided operators are indeed *fast*. For those who are media-aware, and can connect with the many information and social networks that are homing in on niche audiences and connected communities, the potential is awesome.

Chapter Five

An Industry in Flux

How does all of this technology and related social consumers tie into the evolution of the restaurant industry? The simple answer is that the best restaurant chains are also multimillion dollar brands that have passion and creativity, and that purvey something that appeals to the sensual tastes and biological needs of everyone on the planet: food. To this, we can add the incredible proliferation of social media and blogs and the portability of information that comes with smartphones and tablet devices. When we mix in a dash of creativity from the brands, restaurant operators, and local marketers, we have a new recipe for the Food Network 2.0.

Apart from the non-food-specific media I have already mentioned, we are already seeing this happening in the restaurant and dining media. P.F. Chang's spinoff Pei Wei has begun to create its

own online video brand via its YouTube channel "East of Usual,"
focusing on the explorations of a blogger exploring new and exciting Asian culinary treats from around the world. Starbucks also
launched its Starbucks Digital Network in partnership with Yahoo! in
October 2010, offering patrons free wireless connectivity and access
to a broad range of brand-accented content. This proprietary network connects Starbucks' already-loyal clientele to a broad range of
carefully selected news, entertainment, and information channels as
well as Foursquare. The company's total control over its own media
ecosystem gives it unprecedented power to command its brand
message and build customer affinity.

That is merely the tip of the iceberg as major restaurant brands
begin to leverage the ease and cost-effectiveness of podcasting,
WiFi, broadcasting, and social networking technology to transition
from being on the media to being the media. And that media has an
audience. Total the top 25 restaurant brands on Facebook and you
get more than 100 million "likes," as reported by the Restaurant
Social Media Index (www.rsmindex.com). Now let's assume that
this 100 million represents about 40 million actual consumers who
"like" multiple restaurants. What could 40 million motivated consumers do to completely transform the food service landscape?
They could shift politics, create new cultural memes overnight, and

catapult a previously unknown restaurateur into a national sensation in 24 hours!

That was never possible when the media was a top-down behemoth, but it's not that way anymore. The restaurant brands of the future have the power to control the message and its delivery if they choose to master the technology that makes it possible.

However, the changes wrought by mobile media and social networks are a subset of the greater changes in the American dining landscape. The greater sophistication of the U.S. consumer, together with increased expectations created by the fast-casual leaders like Starbucks, is transforming the restaurant industry at its core. The food business has morphed over the past two decades, inaugurating a new and vibrant new paradigm for how consumers will eat out over the next 30 to 40 years. The fast-food industry as represented by McDonald's, Taco Bell, Wendy's and other power players, which has ruled American food culture since the 1960s, is at the threshold of obsolescence.

We are entering the Age of Fast Casual. Some of the evidence:

- According to the Restaurant Industry Tracking Survey of the National Restaurant Association (NRA), 65% of fast-casual operators reported a same-store sales gain between April 2010 and April 2011.

- The NRA also said that 57% of fast-casual operators expected to have higher sales between May and October of 2011, despite the economy.
- According to Technomic's 2011 Top 100 Fast-Casual Chain Restaurant Report, fast casual outpaced the broader restaurant industry in 2010, with the top 100 fast-casual chains growing by 6% to nearly $18.9 billion in revenues.
- Total stores nationwide grew to 15,827, according to Technomic, up 3.9% from 2009.
- Research firm Mintel predicts that the fast-casual segment will exhibit 5% growth per year over the next few years, even accounting for the slow economic recovery.

Incidentally, Panera and Chipotle were number one and number two in sales in 2010. Chipotle's sales boomed a phenomenal 20.7%. Apparently, part of the Chipotle Effect is to have a license to print money for store operators.

At this writing, the recovery from the 2008 recession is fragile and uncertain. The reality is that regardless of the direction the overall economy takes, the restaurant industry will face economic and operational challenges. Economically, fast casual would seem to be on solid footing, as the perception of high quality plus high value should continue driving increased monthly visits to chains in this restaurant segment. Fast casual is still seen as offering excellent value in tough times.

Operationally, things are different. Restaurants will need even more quality workers who can provide the personal service and experience that customers have come to expect. But as more experienced workers drop out of the labor force because they cannot find jobs commensurate with their previous positions, and the new labor force is comprised mainly of young students with little experience and even less desire to work in food service, where will those quality workers come from? A software engineer stinging from a layoff is not going to accept a job at Noodles & Co.

Expansion strategies are on the drawing boards of every executive in the restaurant industry. But I think it unlikely that the lion's share of future growth will come from the national QSR chains. The labor problem is simply prohibitive. Instead, I expect regional and local brands to show the greatest initiative in attracting skilled, passionate workers who can deliver an experience that resonates with consumers, connect to the community, and turn out evangelists.

Difference-making employees will go to the restaurant chains that offer not only better pay and benefits but a hip, classy, personalized working environment. High school seniors are proud to say that they work at Pizza Fusion, a cult-like South Florida chain that is the cool, hip place to hang, or over at Lime Fresh, another South Florida group that serves the too-trendy, including some Kardashians.

It's About Concepts

Don't get me wrong. Brands can and do go global. But in the age of Facebook, Twitter and Yelp, it's extremely difficult to turn customers into raving evangelists—which is what a fast-casual concept needs in order to get big fast—without a local presence and a connection to a local culture. Example: Sushirito in San Francisco, a one-unit concept restaurant, is remaking the idea of sushi as a burrito. That's wonderfully daring, but could it work in Oklahoma City? Maybe, but you would need some big-brand champions to help deliver that unit to profitability. It's hard to build that kind of evangelism when you don't have people on the ground who can rev up local enthusiasm.

There's nothing wrong with this new dynamic, by the way. Change is endemic to the restaurant business; the relative stability that existed with the rise of McDonald's and fast food in general was an anomaly. The industry must accept the fact that as global as we may seem, local is more powerful. The day of the big brand is changing, though it is not coming to a close. That's healthy for our industry. Here's a brief history of the changing of the guard in the restaurant world:

- **Wendy's threatens McDonald's**—Dave Thomas founded the Wendy's chain in 1969 in Columbus, Ohio, and for years Wendy's trailed far behind McDonald's and Burger King among hamburger restaurants. But following a re-tooling of the stores and brand in 1986, Wendy's began its resurgence. In merging with Arby's, adding a menu of healthy options, and making other changes, the chain has grown tremendously, to the point that it is the fifth-largest U.S. restaurant chain, trailing only the Golden Arches, BK, Starbucks, and Subway. As of March 2010, Wendy's Group had more than 6,500 locations around the world, and the company posted 2010 total revenues of $3.4 billion. Perhaps most telling, as of June 2011 the chain had "out-buzzed" both McDonald's and Burger King. According to the YouGov BrandIndex "buzz score," which measures the consumer perception of brands, Wendy's rated a 28.8 buzz score, far above McDonald's 23.1, reflecting consumers' higher opinion of Wendy's quality. In 25 years, Wendy's has gone from also-ran to serious threat to McDonald's and BK's dominance.

- **Burger King slumps**—On the other end of the change spectrum lies Burger King, which has suffered with the slumping economy. Despite operating more than 12,000 stores worldwide and posting $2.5 billion in domestic 2010 sales, the chain is hurting. The company reported a $34.5 million loss for the second half of 2010, and its income slipped $6.2 million in the first quarter of 2011. To add to the chaos, the company was sold in the fall of 2010 to investment group 3G Capital, while CEO John Chidsey stepped down. The overall picture is of a number-two chain that's reeling, but why? Part of the problem may be BK's slowness in moving into healthful food options; in fact, the stores became known for meals that were raging with artery-clogging trans fats. Whatever the reasons, the fact remains that BK now resides below Subway and Starbucks on the QSR pantheon.

- **Subway and Starbucks rise**—On that note, we look at the sandwich maker and the coffee brewer. As of March 2011, Subway passed McDonald's to become the world's largest restaurant chain with (at that time) 33,749 locations. Without question, Subway has leveraged the public's greater interest in healthy fare to grow at an exponential pace. Most impressively, Subway has hit number one in total locations while spotting the Golden Arches a 25-year head start and, not opening its first location until 1965. Then we have Starbucks, the oft-mocked symbol of rapacious capitalist expansion. With more than 17,000 stores worldwide and 11,000 in the United States, the Seattle-based coffee giant is now the number-three QSR brand in the nation, leaping over Wendy's and Burger King to take that spot. This also reflects the desire among many American consumers for healthy food purchased in a welcoming environment from a company with a social conscience via companies like Subway and Starbucks.

Simply put, nothing is static in the restaurant industry. The next big idea is already out there, gestating somewhere away from the bright media lights of New York and Los Angeles. The face of change is not only in the increasingly global nature of our business but also in the challenge of distilling a global message down to a local level and turning it into something authentic and organic that really connects with consumers.

This quality of "making you feel special" is something we all crave from our friends, family members, and the companies we do business with. This is especially true in the "passion" elements of life: food, style, and music. We want to look and feel sexy in that Hugo Boss suit. We want to have the hippest music possible on our iPods. We want to feel like the place we choose to eat both recognizes and reflects our uniqueness. *Passion* is what turns customers into raving, Tweeting, Foursquare-using evangelists who build local brands, and smart restaurant operators find ways to stoke passion.

In the late 1990s I presented several ideas to Starbucks related to introducing a drive-thru that would offer a different sensory experience than what the company was currently delivering. The response? "How can you deliver passion in three minutes in a drive-thru?" That is the right question to ask. Starbucks gets it. I will always remember the coffee-rich smells of the building as I walked down to a drugstore co-housed on the first floor of their corporate offices.

In the years to come, Starbucks integrated drive-thru and has become one of the most successful drive-thru restaurants in America. But that experience is also changing. I have always dreamed that the drive-thru could be the next frontier of dynamic, adaptive sensory experiences for QSR customers. I would like to see Starbucks and other companies evolve the experience completely. The technology to create real innovation is finally available, and best of all, consumers are embracing that technology with the kind of passion that we wish they would bring to their relationships with our restaurants. Brands like Chipotle and Panera have found ways to capture that passion. Doing so throughout the fast-casual industry will require a fearless embrace of radical and disruptive change.

Food as Lifestyle

Hot Tip

If I had to apply a label to fast-casual success stories like Panera, it would be "food-as-lifestyle." That is, for the patrons and the owners of these companies, dining is much more than a refueling stop. It is a holistic part of a complete lifestyle centered on a few essential concepts: speed, convenience, local and personal connection, empowerment through technology, and health. The fastest-growing players in the fast-casual landscape have embraced those ideas to varying degrees and found ways to help consumers relate to them in new ways.

The businesses that have been most effective in this new space are those that understand that what consumers want almost as much as food is *information*—information that they can use to exert influence over their food choices and make the greatest use of their time. That means media, networks, and technology, but it also means an attitude that leaves typical corporate parochialism behind. Rather than erecting corporate firewalls and then hiding operations behind them, Restaurant 2.0 players show all their cards, saying in effect: "Look, this is how we run things! This is where we source our chicken and this is what we pay our employees!" This attitude understands that the customer remains king, and that ceding some power to the customer via Facebook and Yelp does not make the operators of Chipotle any less in charge. It does make them accountable, approachable, and responsive, which is what this new world demands.

What if the world's biggest restaurant brand, McDonald's, were to embrace food-as-lifestyle? What could it do with its billions in revenue if it became more like Starbucks? If McDonald's launched its own information network that informed *local* consumers about *local* health and nutrition opportunities, events, and promotions, I believe this would change everything. Laugh if you will, but the fact remains that the Golden Arches are the leading fast-food brand to cross over to a healthier brand, according a survey of 238,000 consumers by my company, DigitalCoCo.

If McDonald's were to fully embrace healthy choices from the ground up, rather than adding salads and parfaits to its existing unhealthy menu, I believe it would quickly become perhaps the leading food lifestyle brand in the world. That is what will need to happen for these old-guard companies to endure in this age of consumer empowerment, health awareness, and powerful technology. To flourish in an era of agile, consumer-aware fast-casual powerhouses, old-line behemoths like McDonald's must disrupt their proven models and reinvent themselves according to today's new rules.

A new consumer is in the house, one shaped many years earlier by an era of consumer-centric operations. Today she or he is an iPhone wielding, tweet-posting, video-producing media machine. He or she might be pissed off or highly enchanted, but he or she is not ambivalent. What we face today is something that the old-line food purveyors could not have dreamed of: a consumer who has the power to make or break a business, knows he or she has that power, and *likes* it.

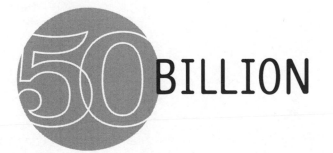

Fast Casual Segment predicted to reach 50 billion in sales by 2017

Chapter Six

Creating Consumer Delight

The era of consumer demand for speed at the expense of health and even choice has come to a close. New consumer demands track the rise of the instant, always-available society. As the Internet inaugurated a global age of accessible information, customers began to flex their muscles and discover that their newfound power could not only influence demand among existing restaurants but also propel the development of the fast-casual industry as a whole.

In earlier years, the customer had little choice or control. Food choice (or the lack of it) was the accepted norm in the restaurant industry. In QSR, the landscape was pretty much burgers, burgers, and more burgers. The birth of new, narrower niche restaurants in cuisines like Mexican, Italian, and Asian matched stride-for-stride the population's increasing demand for greater specialization and greater choice. Consumers began prospecting widely for new dining options where they could find superior value, choice, and quality all in one place.

Enter the fast-casual restaurateur. The consumer's need to feel like their dining establishments "got" them and delivered unique, personalized experiences gave food service entrepreneurs a new area of value that they could begin to leverage in their designs, menus, customer service, and even in their business models. This need to belong to the cool crowd became a new restaurant segment that stood between the speed and questionable quality of fast food and the cost, slowness, and formality of sit-down dining.

Self-Congruent Consumerism

This trend is part of what the July 2009 Research and Markets report Global Consumer Trends: Individualism called "self-congruent consumerism":

"...a trend whereby the image that a person has of her/himself often influences the brand/product choice. By choosing brands with par-

ticular image associations, individuals can communicate to others the type of person they are or want to be seen as."

This is common behavior with products. Consumers for hundreds of years have purchased items in order to advertise a specific quality that they either possess or wish others to think they possess, from the fur coats and diamond stickpins of old to the iPads and Toyota Priuses of today. This has extended into the fast-casual realm because we are, thanks in part to social networking, defined by all of our consumer choices to an unprecedented extent.

Consumers who identify themselves as being "green," healthy, tasteful and hip will gravitate to a fast-casual establishment like Mooyah Burgers, Piada, Sushi Maki, Veggie Grill, or Panera—even if they don't actually possess those qualities. The unconscious intent is that in the same way that holding the new iPhone imparts an air of cool, frequenting such a restaurant will "imprint" the consumer with those aspects that he wants to possess and wants other people to perceive. Consumers who self-identify as blue-collar conservatives might frequent a more traditionally positioned chain such as White Castle because it reflects certain qualities they wish to possess. And so on.

Self-congruent consumerism means that consumers will flock to trends even when they do not understand the implications or facts behind those trends. They'll do so because the trend in question supports their identity. This is why every aspect of the fast-casual experience—environmental design, aural design, menu, social networking, sourcing of ingredients—is so critical to making that initial identity-based connection.

Super Influencers represent the leading targets for brands of the future

Hot Tip

Super Influencers

People often tell me that consumers don't really know what fast casual is. I disagree. They may not understand the business terminology used in the boardroom, but they understand quality, style, and cult-like environments very well. They are also extremely adaptive, so that when a consumer discovers a fast-casual restaurant that gives him or her a delightful experience, he or she is quick to spread the word. The opposite is also true. So to think that consumers don't get what this is all about is rubbish. Most of the time it's the early adopter, who I also call the Super Influencer, who guides, recommends, and even starts trends that others adopt.

Super Influencers are the customers that everyone hopes will fall in love with their business. They are the ones that we try to delight with every aspect of our restaurants, from branding to environmental design. They are very savvy, and they see right through the wannabes—the companies that are trying to do too much too soon or the ones that are being manipulative rather than authentic. These are the people who created fast casual by demanding more choices. I understand Super Influencers because I am one. I'm an early adopter of tech, fashion, and foods. I'm constantly trend-watching and analyzing how we interact with new products and services, especially restaurants.

In their book *The Influentials: One American in Ten Tells the Other Nine How to Vote, Where to Eat, and What to Buy*, authors Jon Berry and Ed Keller assert that the ten percent of Americans who become "tastemakers" are not necessarily celebrities or the super-rich, though those are the ones who get the attention in the tabloids.

Instead, they argue, influentials are the people most likely to talk about their likes and dislikes:

They are not your stereotype of who runs the country. They are not the familiar faces portrayed in the mass media as the change agents in society and the marketplace. Many have achieved material success but they are generally not the richest Americans. They are well educated but generally not the most educated Americans. They are accomplished in their careers but not at the top of industry. You won't often see them on the front page of The New York Times or The Wall Street Journal or on the evening network news. Their homes, recipes, wardrobes and summer reading aren't likely to be parsed in celebrity magazines or on television programs.

In other words, they are regular people who, as the authors make clear, are distributed across a dizzying array of demographic lines. They're not necessarily young and cool, or rich and famous. What influentials typically have in common in that they are actively and widely involved in community, civic, or professional life, have many personal relationships, and are deeply trusted by others. When you give such a person the tools to communicate with thousands on a near-continual basis, such as Facebook and Twitter, you get an influential tastemaker.

Ed Keller is a marketing research expert and the CEO of the Keller Fay Group, a firm specializing in word-of-mouth marketing. Jonathan Berry, former vice president and senior research director for the market research and consulting firm RoperASW, is one of the country's leading consumer-trend analysts. These are two men with their fingers on the pulse of what drives consumer behavior, and their theories, which predate social networking, are nonetheless perfectly in line with its power. If the marketplace created influentials, then social networks gave them a louder voice than ever before.

Design Matters

Super Influencers have also had a profound impact on the design of fast-casual restaurants. These are the same people who gravitate to the iPhone, iPad, and Nissan Leaf because everything about their look and feel is cool, seamless, and stylish. It's no wonder that their tastes have changed how our dining establishments look!

When I walk into a fast-casual restaurant, the subtle design elements that most others don't see are obvious to me—especially if they are ingenious or make the experience memorable. Daring, intuitive, and intelligent store designs can create emotional resonance for consumers that they remember and return for.

Recently I visited my good friend Louis Basile, founder of the Wildflower Bread Company in Phoenix, Arizona. If you are ever near these wonderful restaurants, you must visit one. Louis "gets it." I was touring his newest location, which featured many new design elements that were focused on customer engagement. When I first walked into the restaurant I was met with a half-wall that hid a seating area for guests to wait for friends to join them before they got in line to place an order. It was an honest attempt to serve the social networking impulse, but a misguided one in its execution.

I love meeting people at restaurants for business meetings, but I always find it rude to be seated before they arrive. So this type of area would seem to be a good idea, in theory. The problem was that at this restaurant, the wall hides the party that is waiting. I sat back and observed how customers reacted to this. After watching several groups of diners enter, the most common reaction to the seating area was a blank stare. Instead of seeing the gorgeous "joy and food" message masthead that welcomed diners to the Wildflower, the half-wall caused pause, delay, and the panic you often experience when you arrive and think, "Oh, no, I'm the first one here."

In a fast-casual restaurant, we have to place our order at the counter and in most cases we are not led to a table. So after seeing the same effect with multiple parties, it was clear to me that this design error was causing slowness in the order queue, which in a lunch rush can have a major impact on table turn. But the real impact is that the design could make customers uncomfortable, though the effect would probably not be enough to cause them to not come back. But it will have an impact. Some visitors will ask to meet their companions on the patio or if that's too much trouble, simply go elsewhere. Consumers analyze everything in a dining engagement several times over before they ever select that "favorite" place. They ask numerous questions. Will there be a wait? Is the line too long? Are tables hard to get? What are the Yelp ratings? What are people saying on Facebook or Twitter? Give a Super Influencer a reason to say something less than flattering about your restaurant via the Web or social media and you can negatively impact your brand.

I shouldn't pick on Louis. We had an amazing lunch with great food, which is what Wildflower is really known for. While that is paramount in today's fast-casual business model, the fact is that the space is becoming crowded. "Amazing food" may be becoming as well-worn and empty a brand promise as "fast food" has become in the world of Taco Bell and Hardee's. Ten years ago, we wondered how fast the drive-thru at our favorite QSR haunt would be, because that was the differentiator for fast food. After all, the food was basically all the same quality. Speed was the killer app. But now with lane timers, digital audio systems, and split lane throughput, everyone has a three-minute order-to-delivery time. Speed doesn't get it done anymore.

In fast casual, players like Chipotle and Panera have raised the bar to the point where great food is almost taken for granted. In this environment, food doesn't impress the Super Influencers. It takes a blend of design, technology, and that elusive quality known as "cool" to turn tastemakers into business makers. Consumers are fickle. First we wanted convenient food away from home; hence the evolution of fast food. Then we wanted speed and consistency, which led to McDonald's, Sonic, Burger King and more. Now we want speed and quality and service and cool all in one. How finicky we are! Despite all this, fast food still exists today. It's just taken a form we perhaps did not expect.

Design Meets Technology

Hot Tip

Design is one of the key drivers that engage consumers. You need look no further than Apple for proof that attention to design can change everything. From the debut of the iMac in 1998, design changed the way the company went about product creation. Apple began life as a computer company, trying (and failing) to keep pace with Microsoft. It was only when the company, under the late Steve Jobs, embraced its identity as a consumer products company and began applying its unmatched design brilliance to consumer experiences that its renaissance occurred.

There are many other examples of how design is changing the way people think about products or services. Amazon redesigned online shopping, not so much with beautiful graphics but with a simple customer experience. Shoe company Zappos designed a customer service process that won it raving fans—and eventually resulted in its purchase by Amazon! Chipotle designed itself into the darling of the restaurant industry with a foil-wrapped burrito and a cool, hip feel that made its customers feel healthy and virtuous. Starbucks redesigned the coffee shop. Virgin America redesigned in-flight service, from its glowing purple lighting to its hip crew attire to its quirky, funny, animated safety videos. Design matters.

Design blended with technology can also turn a normal dining experience into something new, changing the way we experience food. Witness the Rainforest Café chain. This is not a fast-casual restaurant, but it has built everything around its design concept of putting customers in the middle of an Amazon rainforest, complete with animatronics and special effects. This creates an "immersion dining" environment that changes how customers perceive the food and themselves. The designed environment has made the Rainforest Café a destination. Chains like the T-Rex Café have followed suit and experienced the same kind of growth.

Technology and the availability of information represent a new frontier for the restaurant operator. This is already happening on the retail side: Walmart recently acquired social tracking company Kosmix—an acquisition that could catapult the company beyond its bargain-basement image. Its goal may be to create boutique retail centers and use real-time data mining of Facebook and Twitter conversations to engage the consumer in a more relevant way—mirroring what fast-casual restaurants like Chipotle have already been doing. This new effort, @WalmartLabs, will change the way business intelligence is gathered and acted upon in the future—much like what my company, DigitalCoCo, is doing by mapping the activity of over 30 million U.S. consumers who are frequent customers of the restaurant industry. The future battlefield for restaurants will be a social media command center plugged into a platform like what we have created in the Restaurant Social Media Index (www.rsmindex.com.) Companies in all segments will look to real-time social data to figure out what to deliver, when to deliver it, and who is demanding it.

Starbucks is also embracing the convergence of design and technology. The company is becoming a media company, as evidenced by the recent launch of the Starbucks Network. This is part of a new stage in brand evolution: total control of the ecosystem from media creation on up. For Starbucks, content is the new drug instead of coffee; the company's goal now is to design the entire engagement with the customer. The sale of coffee is a side effect. Starbucks is rapidly changing direction, a bold and disruptive move in this industry. They have all the assets: density of locations, a ton of cash, and a customer base of people who are key influencers in the community. If Starbucks were to add its own Starbucks Labs to the mix and begin mining data from social networks to drive interactions at their retail centers, they could become a company capable of swaying public policy, and shifting intellect and creativity into places where it is currently lacking.

Design and creativity are the keys to innovation. If America is not innovating creatively, we will fall behind the rest of the world.

The Chipotle Effect

PART II

Chapter Seven

Food Porn

Julia Child couldn't have imagined the food landscape in its current, totally obsessive and celebrity-driven incarnation. The tall, gawky, reedy-voiced author of the classic *Mastering the Art of French Cooking* might have had a hard time even landing her own show in the era of Giada DeLaurentiis, Rachael Ray, and the geek chic of Alton Brown. Today, cooking is sexy and it's big business. Today, millions tune into shows like *Top Chef* and *Iron Chef* and buy books, food, cookware, and much more from major TV chefs-turned-brands like Paula Deen and The Barefoot Contessa.

Food is the new pornography. Americans are fascinated with its sourcing, preparation, seasoning, and in some cases its scope and grotesquerie—witness some of the gastroenterological night-mares that Adam Richman dives into as part of the hit show *Man Vs.*

Food. Local eating has spawned the "locavore" movement. The recession has sparked a new foraged foods craze in which scrounged dandelions, nettles, and fiddleheads become haute cuisine. Slow Food has gone mainstream. All this has created a challenging, exciting, and ever-changing landscape for the fast-casual purveyor. How to remain relevant and authentic when the customer is peering right into the kitchen, pointing, and shouting, "No! Cook this, not that!"

For the Love of Food

Part of the success of fast-casual stalwarts has to go to the Food Network. The Scripps Network-Tribune Company channel is the alpha and omega of the foodie culture, seen by more than 90 million viewers in the United States. The tremendous success of the network's cooking shows and nighttime reality programs such as *The Next Food Network Star* and *Man Vs. Food* has helped to make celebrity megabrands out of the likes of Mario Batali, Bobby Flay, Rachael Ray, Giada DeLaurentiis, and others.

Largely singlehandedly, the Food Network has turned Americans into a nation of food fanatics while educating us as well. But despite its success, the Food Network is largely irrelevant now. The real "food network" that matters is the one composed of a million restaurants with passionate operators, creative culinary minds, sommeliers, nutritionists, and event coordinators. Even the Food Network and its celebrity chefs can't keep up with such a passionate and creative group. With content platforms like Flipboard, Hootsuite, personalized iPad magazine Zite (purchased by CNN), and many others, there are more ways for restaurateurs to speak directly to their customers than ever before.

This content platform establishes the power of local content, as I discussed earlier. Imagine a few local restaurants creating mini-food networks of their own using Twitter feeds, featuring their chefs' inspirations and including coupons, contests, and other in-ducements to get customers in the door to try these new creations! Pair this with the rise of the mobile and two-way news and content aggregators available via smartphones and tablets—POW! Paradigm shift. The future is likely to be a vast network of locally focused culinary news together with hyper-local events, culture, and deals, all delivered via the new class of powerful post-PC devices. Fast-casual operators are and should be ideally positioned to leverage this incredible shift. To move in this world you will have to think like a disrupter and still perform as a highly effective innovator. The new skillset is a super plugged-in executive who embodies change, tech, social, mobile, and social consumer science. It's what I now call the Digital Eco-System Leader.

Health as Mega-Brand

Hot Tip

If local is the next "killer app" in the food world, healthy is its cousin. We have spent the last decade learning about bizarre fusion cuisines, gourmet comfort foods, street truck food, you name it—every chef worth his or her apron is trying to find new ways to leverage a variety of traditions to bring something new to diners. But I believe that the next phase in the cycle is "good for me" dining.

We have, of course, been flirting with healthy dining on a smaller scale for many years. In any city, you will find a selection of successful vegetarian, all-natural, and healthy-choice restaurants. However, health-first fast casual on a *large* scale—the scale of 500 locations and millions in revenues—has so far eluded us. However, the time is ripe. For example, a 2011 study by the *Economic Research Service* of the *U.S. Department of Agriculture* (USDA) revealed that Americans are more aware of the importance of their food choices than ever before. We typically do what is good for us, and whatever that may mean to each individual, increasingly, it means natural, light, low in fat, and short on calories. I have already mentioned LYFE Kitchen as one entry into this space.

This development also puts fast casual in position to outpace fast food and casual dining segments, which have become indelibly associated with food that has little or no health or nutritional value. As we are beginning to understand just how our bodies interact with food and how pivotal diet is to overall wellness, the availability of healthful food in a fast-casual setting is becoming a powerful competitive edge.

Consider Whole Foods Market in the grocery segment. The Austin, Texas, powerhouse has grown at an astonishing rate in a comparatively short time by taking the science and sustainability of healthful, organic, natural food to a level that makes it easy for consumers to understand. Whole Foods, which was founded in 1980, employs more than 58,000 people and operates more than 300 stores in the United States. The company had total revenues in 2010 of about $9 billion and regularly wins awards for environmental sustainability and for being one of the best companies to work for. Clearly, opportunity exists in the market defined by aware, educated, health-conscious consumers.

My prediction is that we are on the cusp of the era of food that is both good and good for us. More important, the Fast Food Era is winding down. Food that is high in fat, sodium, and calories, with little or nothing to recommend it other than its speed of delivery and low cost, will fade from the scene. Of course, there remains the argument that better food is more expensive, but is it? Does terrible food that may cost less at the counter but that contributes to obesity and heart disease really cost less in the long run? Consumers are beginning to value food differently. They are showing this with the growth of Whole Foods and the move toward fast casual.

Fast-casual dining is more expensive than fast-food dining, so the only answer to the double-digit growth of the segment is that fast casual is providing something else, something beyond low cost, that consumers demand. That something is not just value but values. Fast casual is seen as reflecting core values of today's tech-empowered, younger consumer: health, sustainability, and corporate responsibility, among others. Because sharp fast-casual operators have spun their brand stories around such commodities as locally sourced meats and hormone-free dairy, posted calorie totals, and built open kitchens where customers can see vegetables being freshly chopped, they attract not only increasing numbers of health-conscious patrons but intense loyalty. "Healthy," "local," and "connected" will be the key trio behind the Chipotles and Paneras of the next decade.

The same people who led the tech and design revolutions will lead the healthy dining revolution: creative, passionate entrepreneurs. But there will be another group at work as well: the celebrity chefs who we got to know through the Food Network. They are waking up and discovering that they have valuable brands, too—brands that transcend the Food Network and that can be exploited. These brands, as I'll discuss, are already changing the food landscape.

 Fooding

iFood

Empowerment is the word of the day in the food business. Customers have the power now, not restaurateurs. Certainly, a new Tom Douglas eatery can make hearts flutter in Seattle, but by and large, the consumer is in charge because of technology. Combine the incredible power of the iPhone, iPad, Android smart phones, services like Yelp and Urbanspoon, and of course Facebook and Twitter, and you get a near-constant flow of bits describing bites.

That energy has upended the traditional power structure of food by handing the masses the means to decide whether restaurants live or die by means of their tweets, updates, and reviews. More than that, consumers are educating each other and flagging their exciting new finds—eateries, chefs, cuisines. Now, so-called "augmented reality" applications allow a smart phone user to aim his camera at a streetscape and see a constellation of menus, reviews, and notes left by both business owners and customers. Apps like Oink and Pinterest are just the beginning of "iFooding"—cataloging and curating not just restaurants but food in real time, based on genuine customer experience. Think of a kind of a cross between Foodspotting, Yelp and Foursquare. Information is everywhere, and if that has somewhat blunted the raw sense of discovery that comes with trying a new restaurant sight unseen, it has empowered people to reward their favorites with authentic acclaim and great success.

This environment has led to a new phenomenon: the celebrity chef as rock star, even in the fast-casual realm. Star chefs have discovered that the start-up costs are lower and the franchising and licensing revenue potential is vastly higher in turning their personal brands into fast-casual chains. Wolfgang Puck was the first major superstar chef to go this route with his Wolfgang Puck Express and Wolfgang Puck To Go stores, which have 48 locations at airports and in affluent regions of Los Angeles and other cities. But now many other big names have gotten into the fast-casual act:

- Bobby Flay—James Beard Award winner and star of shows like *Food Network Star* and *Throwdown!* opened his concept burger restaurant, Bobby's Burger Palace, to highlight ten regional hamburger styles. It's now a chain of six locations in the mid-Atlantic states and has been received very positively online and by the media.

• Rick Melman—The founder of Chicago-based Lettuce Entertain You Enterprises has made a habit of launching creative new restaurant brands with equally creative names: Ben Pao, Big Bowl, Café Ba-Ba-Reeba!, Everest, Foodlife, Mity Nice Grill, Mon Ami Gabi, Nacional 27, R.J. Grunts, Foodese, and Wow Bao. With nearly 80 locations combined around the country, the eateries generate annual sales of about $350 million.

• Danny Mayer—The founder of the Union Square Café and the CEO of the Union Square Hospitality Group, whose restaurants and chefs have earned an unheard-of 19 James Beard awards, ventured into fast casual in 2004 with the opening of Shake Shack, a food kiosk in New York's Madison Square Park, serving Chicago-style hot dogs, burgers, frozen custard, wine and beer. Now, Shake Shack boasts locations in highly influential and global communities like Miami, where the restaurant is located on the famed Lincoln Road on South Beach.

• Rick Bayless—Beard Award winner Bayless, a bestselling cookbook author and promoter of Mexican cuisine, has the distinction of opening one of the few Mexican fine dining restaurants in the country, Tobolobampo. He also dove into fast casual with Xoco, a purveyor of Mexican street food that, according to Bayless' website, features "contemporary expressions of Mexico's most beloved street food and snacks: hot-from-the-fryer churros and flaky empanadas; frothy Mexican hot chocolate (ground from Mexican cacao beans right in our front window!); warm, crusty tortas (Mexican submarine sandwiches); and made-to-order caldos (meal-in-a-bowl soups) that feature everything from roasted vegetables to seafood to pork belly."

The superstar chefs had many motivations to go fast casual: profit, the desire to stretch their talents into more populist grub, and freedom from the starched-linen sensibilities of fine dining. Whatever the reasons, the result has been that new cuisines and cultures have been revealed to consumers, creating demand not only for more restaurants serving those same types of food but for the raw ingredients that consumers could use to prepare the same foods at home.

Authenticity and Street Cred

Hot Tip

The rapid rise of food truck culture has followed the same arc. Not long ago, food trucks were the ghettos of urban cuisine, home to soggy burritos and questionable cleanliness, patronized only by hungry construction workers. Not any more. Now, in cities from Seattle and Austin to Kansas City and Los Angeles, food trucks are a big, big deal. They deal in everything from Korean fusion BBQ to fresh soups to Thai and Greek food, meeting the public's craving for cheap, high-quality food in a super-casual setting. This street food sensibility, which captures a sense of local authenticity, is reflected in many new fast-casual offerings.

The essence of Food Truck culture is serving as a model for newer fast-casual offerings, as well as restaurants in other parallel segments. In a world where local and real are the truest currency, nothing is more local and has more credibility with the urban demographic than a cuisine that grew up step-by-step from consumer demand. This is enhanced by the fact that food trucks are rarely in the same location twice, rarely make it easy for consumers to locate or order food, and provide minimal, if any, seating. How, then, has the Food Truck scene grown so rapidly, despite the comparative lack of fancy dining environments and technology? Could it be that local connection, quality, and a non-corporate feel trump the carefully crafted, focus-grouped dining experience of some of today's hottest fast-casual entries?

In a word, yes. Restaurants that "keep it real" and bring genuine local food, conceived and made by local cooks, to local fans will usually win out in the social networking age. In times past, when advertising and branding dollars determined market share, these businesses and chefs would usually be relegated to niches or swallowed up, but no more. Today, technology has leveled the playing field. Trucks, street food, and regional peculiarities may wind up with a great deal more staying power than all but the most brilliantly conceived brands.

The Evolution of the Food Scene

Take the public awareness (and outrage) generated by works such as *Fast Food Nation* and the documentary *Super Size Me*. Mix in the hyper-local sensibility of Slow Food and the locavore movements. Bring to a boil over public anger at fast-food restaurants that serve high-fat food in huge portions designed to manipulate customers into eating more. What you get is a radical shift in the direction of the food industry.

Foodie Nation continues to thrive and grow. Magazines such as the regional *Edible* publications rhapsodize about local, fresh, organic, and sustainable foods. Farmers markets and Community Supported Agriculture (CSA) farm shares are springing up everywhere. Empowered by their technology and given a voice, consumers are demanding more choices—and getting them. In an environment

increasingly concerned with sustainability, organic foods, and transparency, it's not surprising that Chipotle has thrived. The popular
YouTube video "Back to the Start," created by Chipotle, shows how
the industry is making the transition back to locally sourced ingredients and high value—producing simple good food versus selling the
board room-designed approach to culinary nirvana.

In this environment, what consumers want from their dining establishments is much less clear than in years past. In the
past, good food and good service were the alpha and omega of the
hit restaurant. Quality food and service still matter of course, but
they are not enough to create a hit-making buzz. Chefs face more
evolved palates and customers who can get real-time information on
the sourcing and provenance of ingredients and the background of
kitchen staff.

In the new reality, great food and good service are no longer the
Holy Grail in a review. Any competently run restaurant can deliver
those. Hit businesses must blend quality with creative and sometimes audacious blends of ingredients, flavors, and cuisines. They
must have daring, risky presentations. They must be up front about
where they get everything, from their beef and eggs to the flowers
on the table centerpieces. And they must leverage technology for
all it's worth from reservations to having their own smart phone

and iPad apps. It will always be possible for the extraordinary few to thrive based only on incredible food and peerless service, but for the other 99% these other factors will make the difference between prosperity and failure.

In a way, this changing landscape is like the one that saw fast casual rise in the early 1990s and throw fast food for a loop. Now, this former upstart controls the fastest growing segment in a $600 billion industry. Today, the new stage of evolution will force a new generation of fast-casual restaurants to up their game or perish.

Acceptance of Fast Casual

Hot Tip

In 2011, the National Restaurant Association (NRA) forecast that consumers would continue to seek new options, new flavors, and new cuisines, driving the future of how we as an industry evolve. To tell the truth, I fear for the casual dining segments that can't adapt to this new reality. Even some players in the fine dining segment will begin to lose some baby boomer customers as their prime source of revenue in 2016. That's when the Millennials—those born between 1980 and 2000—will displace the boomers as the new center of power in consumer spending. Do you really think a wired, fast-moving, information-saturated 30-year-old Facebook employee will spend his dining dollars at Morton's? Neither do I.

I am often asked what the next real innovation for the restaurant industry will be. After all, all we really do is provide food and service along with a splash of experience, right? Answer: Foodie Nation will begin interacting with restaurants at the fundamental level, the level of the food in its purest form. Consumers will become even more educated about our businesses and continue to demand higher quality ingredients, new fusions, and more choices. The entrepreneurs who can provide these things will own the future.

Restaurant operators and companies will have to fight to maintain their connection to this new consumer. It will not come automatically or as a birthright. Social networks, online entertainment, mobile media, and more will compete for the attention of the Fast Casual 2.0 customer. Local and healthy will be critical as restaurants reach out; the sourcing and provenance of the food will be as important as the taste of the final product. Creativity is the new currency. Mom and pop operators will not get a free pass, either. They have always had an edge in authenticity and local connection, and that will not change. But every restaurant owner will be required to engage in brand development, with the tools more accessible than ever. Today, a brand can rise to prominence on the basis of a blog, some social networking strategy, and a great website. Ten years ago, it took a team of 20 people, two years and a few million dollars to develop a dominant regional restaurant brand. Now two people can do it in months with a fraction of the capital with Twitter, a Facebook page, and a mobile app for $25,000.

The NRA report's predictions essentially anoint a new kind of restaurateur as the future of this business. This new breed is built around big-idea people who have a vision of what culinary delight really means and how to communicate that to the consumer. Mooyah Burgers and Fries in Dallas is an example. This brand is nicely positioned in the crowded "better burger" segment, with the ability to grow. Led by Rich Hicks and Todd Istre, and shepherded through expansion by Alan Hixon (who built the Freebirds Burritos concept from nothing to a power player in Fresh Mex) the company is one to keep an eye on. These are the new restaurateurs of the future who are thinking way outside the box and are always in innovation mode.

Many restaurants in this segment are taking the path of Five Guys, the direction of the burger chains of yesteryear. Though Five Guys is bigger and has a powerful consumer base, my prediction is that they are going in same direction as the mighty McDonald's: obscurity. Mooyah continues to offer the satisfying experience of a great decadent burger but with a model that allows them to flex to meet the needs of the evolving consumer. The innovative store designs and kid-friendly atmosphere are just two examples. They are setting new standards for customer service, and personal engagement in their stores is interactive and fun. Along with superlative food, you have a winning combination. Expect some new fresh menu options and some innovation in interaction from this brand.

Our best efforts to date involve providing good food with a splash of experience. I believe the future will be in telling the story of the food, not just in the delivery of the food and service. Chipotle already does this very well in low-tech fashion by putting engaging stories and narratives on things like cups and napkins. Via in-store materials, menus, point-of-purchase displays, mobile media, or the Web, restaurants will have to reach out to Foodie Nation and create informed consumers who appreciate how their food is sourced and understand the significance of cruelty-free, hormone-free, and so on.

In order to thrive, restaurants will need to create their own publishing channels. We see this, of course, with foodie blogs, Facebook pages, Twitter feeds, and SMS messaging, but it will carry forward into other media. Just as the rise of the Food Network and the bevy of celebrity chefs and food reality shows that litter the landscape have taken "food porn" mainstream, the need to connect with Foodie Nation on a more personal level will drive a new demand for authenticity and transparency in the industry.

Time-Shifting

Chapter Eight

Time-Shifting and the Death of Drive-Thru Nation

Time shifting is a concept developed by Michael Tchong, the founder of Ubercool. His theory is that we all look for solutions that help us control our time. Just about every decision we make is based on how much time something takes. What time do we go to beat the rush at a restaurant or get the best table?

Time shifting helped create the entire fast-casual segment. We all knew what it was to go through a three-minute drive-thru experience. So speed has clearly been on our minds for a while. But what changed? What made us believe that speed, quality, and price could all be maximized at the same time? It was the Internet, of course. It has made us a time-shifting nation.

However, nothing can be sped up infinitely. What is the tipping point for time shifting? I don't know this, but I suspect it's some time away. The potential of mobile and tablet computing platforms has barely begun to be tapped; in just ten years, the technology will be so advanced and woven into our everyday lives that time will become even more malleable and valuable than it is today. With mobile computing and the cloud, 24x7 connectivity has been realized. We already have the power to communicate, share info, research, and initiate action on a huge array of needs in our lives in seconds and on the move, from confirming a visit from a plumber to locating and booking a table at the best Cuban restaurant in Miami's South Beach. We text, tweet, Skype, surf, update, read ebooks, and watch movies on live streaming all while on the subway en route to our favorite downtown district. Nothing is impossible to the generation that has embraced the potential of this mobile technology, and their food providers had better keep up.

What will happen in the future of the restaurant business? Time will continue to compound. Much like Moore's Law showed the exponential increase in microchip power, time shifting will continue to force us to evolve in how we work, carry on relationships, and feed ourselves. Restaurants are not exempt. And while these days time shifting is mostly an experience of the affluent, this will change as well. The cost of tech always drops. Within a few years, lower-cost devices that carry as much power as today's iPhone or iPad will appear on the market, opening time shifting potential to everyone.

How the Shift Began

The shift in time perception and consumer thinking that began as far back as 2002, with the rise of blogs and the availability of mobile media, hit high gear with the publication of Eric Schlosser's bestselling book, *Fast Food Nation*. Until that time, consumers had already begun to use email and text messaging to spread the positive or negative word about a restaurant, but the larger narrative about what was in the food we were eating did not take hold. *Fast Food Nation* changed that.

The book, a scathing exposé of the fast-food industry in particular and the food-industrial complex in general, outraged both food industry executives and consumers. Industry heavy hitters were furious because of the book's unremittingly negative portrayal of Big Food. Schlosser's portrait depicted food companies as using every tactic in the book to manipulate the brains and taste buds of John Q. Public to get him to stuff as much high-fat, high-salt, high-calorie junk into his mouth as possible. Worse were the portrayals of the food-processing plants where the beef and chicken originated.

The New York Times wrote that the book would "...not only make you think twice before eating your next hamburger, but it will also make you think about the fallout that the fast food industry has had on the social and cultural landscape." For the industry, Fast Food Nation marked the beginning of the end of business as usual.

Consumers for their part were furious about the stories of chemical augmentation, disgusting slaughterhouses, and environmental degradation. They didn't stop patronizing fast-food establishments, but they began to demand a better experience in return for their continued loyalty. For example, the drive-thru had long since lost its novelty and allure. Consumers saw a drive-thru lane as a necessity but moaned about the long lines of cars and the endless wait to get their orders. The design of the drive-thru—a single lane with a two-way speaker and menu board followed by a window where you paid and got your food—had not really evolved since the 1950s.

Consumers learned how to avoid the poorly designed drive-thru lines and began to ask for new ways to get their lunch. McDonald's adaptation to this demand helped create the first dual-lane drive-thru models that dotted the landscape in the mid 1990s. These helped to speed up the consumer's visit and keep them connected to the fast-food giant they had grown to love but distrusted.

Catering to the time-poor consumer became the raison d'etre for many fast-food chains. Even as they were expressing their new knowledge and hyper-awareness of quality food through blogs and foodie clubs, Americans were also busier than ever, pressed for time from every direction. When they had time for Slow Food, they flocked to it—but they rarely had that time. Instead, they worked to pick up time in every area of their lives. Food quality and sourcing became a secondary issue for the time-pressed consumer.

Technology stepped in to compress the perception of acceptable time. Once, in the days of the 14.4 dialup modem, waiting five minutes for a file to download had been acceptable. Now, broadband Internet meant that consumers flew into a rage when a PDF took more than three seconds to download. Online banking, travel booking, real estate research, and Google reduced the perception of how long we should be willing to wait for something. Our lives became stuck on fast-forward. This new urgency diminished the importance of the drive-thru. What had begun as a timesaving convenience had become a time-wasting ordeal.

Though today drive-thru still represents 60 percent of the fast-food business, the writing is on the wall. Consumers will soon seek new alternatives to pulling into a ten-car lineup for the privilege of waiting as long as 15 minutes to place an order. The burden is shifting to technology innovators to power the fulfillment of orders at Internet speed via the Internet, mobile media, and social networks.

Hot Tip

Fast Casual Nation

Into this environment came the roaring expansion of the fast-casual segment with the opening of new signature restaurants from players such as the celebrity chefs I discussed in the last chapter. Thanks to the Fast Food Nation backlash as well as concerns about the obesity epidemic, dissatisfaction with fast food was on the rise. Fast casual represented a middle ground between jammed fast-food drive-thru lines and the pricier, more time-consuming casual dining experience of chains like Applebee's and The Olive Garden. Here was a choice that consumers could embrace: quick, cost-effective, and tastier than the burgers and tacos they were used to.

Concepts began to defy the norms of restaurant design, with segments that boasted a higher-end dining feel as well as those that mimicked bakeries and delis. Boston-based Au Bon Pain and Boston Market were among the first to really rock the boat in their segments, turning the tables on bakeries and KFC, respectively. In the Los Angeles area, upstarts in the "Fresh Mex" space and even early players in gourmet burgers such as The Habit began to get some traction with consumers.

A world that just a few decades earlier had consisted of basically two levels—fine dining on one end, greasy spoon diners and fast food on the other—had become increasingly subdivided with casual dining and fast casual. And with the nation becoming ever busier yet more concerned about the health effects of what it put in its mouth, it was clear that fast casual was becoming the new go-to cuisine of the twenty-first century.

Fast Casual, the Culture

In reality, fast casual is more than a dining model. It's a cultural ethos that's reflected in many institutions that serve the public. Its basic tenets are universal: high quality; high convenience; a casual, informal tone; lowered or eliminated barriers between the service provider and the consumer; a compelling design and sensory experience; and exceptional value.

Fresh Mex really led the way into this cultural shift, which makes sense. Mexican food restaurants have thrived and taken root in Southern California, a mecca of self-reinvention. So when Baja Fresh began to challenge the established models of the street tacquerias that still dot Los Angeles, its vision led the way. This book may be named after Chipotle, but Baja Fresh actually made some of the earliest inroads toward the fast-casual model that we know today. Jim and Linda Magglos opened the first Baja Fresh in 1990 in Newbury Park, California, based on the motto, "No microwaves, no can openers, no freezers, no lard and no MSG." This fresh-food approach helped the chain grow from 45 locations in 1998 to nearly 250 when Wendy's International acquired it in 2002.

Baja Fresh helped inaugurate some of the classic fast-casual hallmarks that Chipotle and others would later perfect: fresh ingredients prepared onsite, a fast-moving line that revealed an open kitchen, healthy options, and a pleasing, clean, open design more akin to casual sit-down restaurants than to fast food.

The origins of the Better Burger segment are hazier. The Habit actually began in Santa Barbara in 1969 but did not actually go mainstream fast casual until the early 1990s. Five Guys jumped on the fast-casual bandwagon in 2002 when they began to really ramp-up in the Washington, D.C., area. The bottom line is that the evolution of fast-casual culture is like the evolution of Homo sapiens: there are a lot of key moments but no one origin point. In reality, the tide was turning toward a new consumer culture as far back as the 1980s. However, the consumer was still following the fast-food model and would really take another 20 years to make a wholesale shift into what we now know as fast casual.

When that shift occurred, however, it was pervasive. Fast casual is changing more than the restaurant industry. It is impacting a wide range of industries that have become more conscious about reaching out to their customers and revitalizing their brands by creating more experiential environments that are still affordable. Take the boutique hotel industry, which has rolled out its own fast casual-style brands in perfect lockstep with the fast-casual restaurant segment.

Kimpton Hotels is a collection of eclectic, avant-garde boutique hotels founded in 1981 by William Kimpton. Kimpton Hotels—the company also maintains two sub-brands, Hotel Monaco and Hotel Palomar—are not as affordable as, say, a Holiday Inn Express, but they are highly unique in design and amenities and offer a trendy, stylish feeling both in their rooms and their signature bars, which are marketed as edgy and upscale. For a cost far below that of a Ritz-Carlton or Four Seasons, Kimpton guests can sleep in desirable neighborhoods of major cities and enjoy creative, highly original amenities.

Hyatt Place is the Hyatt Corporation's entry into the fast-casual hotel space. Trying to appeal to today's younger, faster paced, tech-savvy business traveler, the owner of the venerable Hyatt brand created a hotel that's more casual and sleeker in design, with more technology and more social gathering space than a typical hotel. Guests are encouraged to bring their own meals into the common space, linger, watch big-screen TVs, and enjoy amenities like high-speed WiFi for free. Luxury is still desirable, but Hyatt Place and Kimpton get it: the new consumer has so many choices and so much information that he or she has all the power. They represent the evolution of hotels.

Banking is no different. ING is serving up all new style locations that have no tellers, offering more DIY banking with a Starbucks look and feel. Other banks are retaining their tellers but designing interior spaces more akin to boutiques. The fact is that consumers are done being subservient. They want comfort, attention, quality service, and convenient technology in their dining, banking, and lodging—and from just about every other important segment of daily life. Smart companies know that if they don't provide it, some-one else will.

Fast casual, more than anything, is a change in how consumers engage with their service providers. Health care is next, as technol-ogy and information become more readily available and consumers become more aware of the myriad elements that impact their health and their health care. Eventually, the relentless power of the in-formed consumer will force the vast medical industry to change how it delivers its products and services—only to the betterment of care, in my opinion.

Every aspect of this fast-casual revolution has been driven by the incredible growth of the Internet—first wired, then wireless, and now in the "cloud." Knowledge is power, and that information made freely available with fast access is giving society the means to learn and evolve at an alarming rate of speed. It was only in 1995 that the World Wide Web became a household name. English physicist Tim Berners-Lee had begun developing the idea of a hypertext-based network of computers to speed information sharing among researchers while working at CERN, the European Particle Physics Laboratory in Geneva, Switzerland.

But not until Lee created HTML—Hyper Text Markup Language—did it begin to become clear that the Internet could become an unlimited repository of human knowledge. Since Lee launched the very first Web page in 1991, the Internet ecosystem has evolved at light speed (with the careful guidance of Lee's World Wide Web Consortium, or W3C) from AOL and dialup through Java and Flash, on to broadband and WiFi, and on to 3G and 4G mobile networks, cloud infrastructure, mobile apps, and incredibly powerful databases. Today, it is a tool that democratizes much of the world and makes much of its vast power available to anyone with a laptop and a wireless device. It would be astonishing if this amazing resource had not transformed how humans think about commerce, information, service, and time.

The Birth of the Cool

Hot Tip

However, what I don't think anyone expected was the cultural war that would emerge from the rise of fast casual. The restaurant segment was very young, and just as young people will be imprudent and reckless in their desire to be cool, the new chains were determined to break away from the stodgy corporate images of McDonald's, Jack in the Box, and the rest, and be hipper, cooler, and edgier. They were after a new consumer: Generation X and Generation Y folks who were joined at the hip with their mobile devices, working at Internet start-ups and in many ways defining the new Internet era in American culture. Rather than try to outspend the deep-pocketed corporate chains, the fast-casual purveyors decided to out-brand them instead.

Starbucks was one of the most successful fast-casual brands to capitalize on this sense of youthful élan. That makes sense; after all, it already had the hip, urban coffee house vibe, even in the days when all its stores looked the same. And despite the fact that the chain has largely struck out with its food products, Starbucks has managed to convince the nation that it needs a four-dollar latte. The company was in the perfect zone at the perfect time to capture the zeitgeist of the dotcom era. Its stores were abundant in places like Seattle, Portland, and San Francisco, where the Internet gold rush was hot. Young entrepreneurs would gather in Starbucks locations at all hours with their laptops, working through their business plans, preparing Power-Points, and loading up on caffeine for big fundraising presentations. Starbucks became a symbol of this young, vibrant, smart, tech-savvy scene, and when the bubble collapsed in 2000, the coffee kept on flowing.

I like to compare the ascendance of the irreverent, hipster fast-casual segment over the old-school fast-food chains to the war between Apple and Microsoft. In this corner, we have the huge, old-school corporate titan, slow moving and set in its ways. That's Microsoft, but it could just as easily be McDonald's or Taco Bell. For years, Microsoft thrived by being the biggest kid on the block. Sure, it innovated new ways to develop and deliver office pro-ductivity software, but its success was built largely on its aggressive business model and competitive strategy: signing agreements with PC makers to put its Windows operating system on the desktops of 90 percent of the world's personal computers. That dominance positioned Microsoft to be the main player in the coming information revolution—and pretty much made them the only game in town when it came to computer and office soft-ware decisions.

In comparison (though it may seem funny now that it's the world's most valuable corporation by market cap), Apple was a young, hip upstart. The company that broke the mold of the PC with the Macintosh and its famous "1984" commercial had become a struggling niche player in the 1990s. It had millions of devoted fans but seemed unable to keep up with the Microsoft powerhouse. When Steve Jobs came back in 1997 to take over the leadership of the company he co-founded, Apple was on the verge of failure.

However, things soon changed. Just as agile, creative, and young fast casual shocked the staid fast-food giants with their store designs, food offerings, and aggressive marketing, Apple stunned archrival Microsoft with a series of counterintuitive plays in the computing space. First came the iMac in 1998, which reinvented the way PCs were supposed to look and revived Apple's image as an innovator. A few years later came the iPod and iTunes, which managed to do something no other company had been able to do: create a pleasing, popular, and profitable music download ecosystem. Then in 2007 came the move that shook the world: Apple's debut of the iPhone. With the debut of this beautifully designed product, the Cupertino, California, company instantly became the leading innovator in mobile computing platforms—a position it has solidified with the release of the wildly successful iPad.

Microsoft, for all its might and money, has floundered ever since. Ill-equipped to innovate in the same way as Apple and far more strict about corporate hierarchy, the Redmond, Washington, company tried and failed to put out a mobile phone operating system and tablet operating system that could begin to compete with Apple's intuitive, gorgeous products. More important, Microsoft's brand went from being perceived as cutting-edge to being stuck in the past, unable to overcome its own size and complexity in order to offer the truly innovative. Though it remains a powerhouse with a very large computer market share, Microsoft is losing ground to Apple. Because the company has a huge installed base of Windows users, its market share of PC operating systems remains above 70%. But in mobile devices, where the future of consumer computing lies, Microsoft is barely even a niche player, with a market share of around three percent, while Apple is at 20 percent and growing.

It's easy to extend the metaphor of Microsoft versus Apple out to fast food versus fast casual. On one hand, you have a still-strong fast-food segment that has attracted even more business during the recession. On the other hand, daring, nontraditional players from Chipotle to Panera to Firehouse Subs to Sweetgreen to Stacked (a new burger concept in southern California where patrons use iPads to place orders) are grabbing a bigger and bigger share of the consumer food dollar and making the longtime fast-food giants very nervous. That is driving change in the fast-food space (witness McDonald's and its McCafe, done to take back market share from Starbucks). As some of the fast-casual rebels become bigger, slower corporations themselves, will they in turn lose ground to small, shockingly creative rivals? We have already seen another round of fast-casual entries from majors like Wendy's, IHOP, and Red Robin, just to name a few. Can they recreate the fast-casual spirit with the speed and force of monster brands, or is there something more to winning consumer hearts than being big and having a concept? This is a billion-dollar question.

Organic Growth

With the rise of the tech-savvy, cool fast-casual chains came changes in how consumers interacted with the brands that provided their food. From the iPhone to Yelp and Twitter, I have discussed some of these in detail. But concurrently with this revolution began a new era of choice and word-of-mouth marketing that drove the growth and evolution of fast-casual chains.

For years, fast casual had been the product of personal passion plays like Steve Ells's decision to open his first Chipotle in a Denver university district. Then, as the years passed and the financial stakes became greater, the segment became more attractive to venture investors, and small companies became more like their former corporate rivals. Now, as social media and mobile communications technology have proliferated, those technologies and the lifestyles they fueled have become powerful motivating factors in the growth and shaping of fast-casual chains.

One example is The Melt, the grilled cheese concept restaurant launched by Jonathan Kaplan, creator of the Flip Camera. Kaplan has huge plans to have 500 locations nationally by 2015, and part of this optimism stems from his use of mobile tech in order to be as customer-friendly as possible. Working with a high-powered team that includes chef Michael Mina and advisors from Apple and Sequoia Fund, Kaplan has already opened his first locations around tech-savvy San Francisco. He plans to use mobile technology there to power fast ordering and pickup. The customer will order and pay via the Melt mobile app for iPhone or iPad, or on the Web, but he or she doesn't have to specify a pickup time or location. Instead, the restaurant's systems send the customer a Quick Response, or QR code. This makes food production and delivery customer-driven.

When the customer decides it's time to get the food, he or she arrives at the restaurant, scans the QR code that was sent at the time of the order, and the grilled cheese of choice then goes on the grill, taking less than a minute to cook. The customer picks up the order without having to wait in line. This is a huge breakthrough in food service: congruent not only with how consumers perceive their own role as drivers of innovation but also in line with their passion for technology and respectful of their desire to have maximum time flexibility. It's a perfect example of technology, demand, and lifestyle propelling business, instead of the other way around.

Another chain, this one more established, that is defying the traditional manner of growth and development is Five Guys Burgers and Fries. The Arlington, Virginia-based chain has built a fast-growing burger brand (more than 750 stores in 40 states) on a quirky, family-based culture. The company really is a mom-and-pop operation, run by Jerry and Janie Murell since its creation in 1986. All of their five sons now also work in the family business, becoming the eponymous "five guys" in the company name.

By embracing homespun touches such as not using timers in its kitchen (saying that "real cooks know when the food is done"), eschewing national advertising, and stacking bags of raw potatoes near the customer lineup areas, Five Guys has gone to the opposite extreme of The Melt. It has effectively positioned itself as low-tech, simple, and honest. This anti-technology stance gives the company a pleasing brand identity that has made it a highflyer in fast casual and one of the most talked-about brands on the social networks.

Given these examples, one could say that while growth in the segment is still driven by investor strategies, exhaustive market research and carefully calibrated design and menu choices, it is also driven more than ever by a combination of consumer tastes and lifestyles and the peculiar passions of company founders, who launch their one-location empires on nothing more than the sweat of their brows and their unique vision of what a dining experience should be.

If Drive-Thru Nation rose to prominence on the backs of a fast-food experience that was numbingly identical and predictable, then the future of quick-service dining appears to be organic, diverse, and unconventional.

Chapter Nine

The Birth of Fast Casual

The hip, cool, techie vibe that has helped to make fast casual such a formidable player in the ultra-competitive restaurant space is no accident. It has been cultivated since the beginnings of the idea of a middle ground between fast food and casual dining. I know, because I was there to see the idea emerge. In fact, I was something of a midwife to the entire concept.

The mashup of fast food and casual dining was one I struggled with. Years ago, when I worked closely as a consultant with many of the fast-food giants as well as many of the emerging hybrid restaurants, I had the revelation that this hybrid style would in fact replace fast food one day.

In 1996, as I presented in New York in front of several industry analysts on the topic of fast food and its future, I reluctantly mentioned the new hybrid model that I saw evolving into a critical player in the industry. These insurgents were blazing across the skies with unprecedented food quality and speed, combining those factors with quasi-industrial designs, daringly original menu concepts, computer and Internet technology, and fairly affordable prices. This seemed to me like a killer combination that could threaten the primacy of the fast-food titans. But many of the analysts that were there that day didn't want to hear about this hybrid style of dining; they wanted me to comment on the amazing growth in QSR/fast food and the rapid rise of Oklahoma's Sonic Drive-in chain, which I was working with closely on several technology fronts.

I had a few slides in my presentation that mentioned the new hybrid fast-casual model, and even some pictures suggesting ways that this fresh design and service ethos could become a viable model for the future evolution of fast food. Remember, this was 1996, a time when the Internet was just cutting its teeth and the dot bomb was just a glint in the eye of Silicon Valley. Everything seemed possible to me, yet the assembled executives hadn't really discovered the power of disruption.

I knew what I was talking about. I had spent years working with Microsoft in the development of Point of Sale (POS) systems designed to help the fast-food industry track and speed up the process of getting food into the hands of customers more cost-effectively. Unfortunately, my expertise didn't change the fact that most of the people in my audience did not want to hear my insistence on the potency of the new paradigm. The group grew restless with my persistent suggestions that the fast-food industry needed to change and could learn from the super-entrepreneurs launching new restaurant brands. The powers that be didn't want to hear it. Instead, they demanded more information, facts, and figures on how technology would make them more efficient and more profitable than ever. It was a major vision FAIL.

Coining the term
Fast Casual

To Coin a Phrase

Finally, frustrated with the denial in the room, and feeling the pressure to give this new hybrid business model a name so they would take it more seriously, I blurted out what I thought was the natural name for such a new hybrid restaurant: part fast food, part casual dining = Fast Casual. A hush fell over the crowd, at least in my mind. A new term for modern dining was coined.

After I returned home later that week, it dawned on me that the explosion of fast-casual dining could in fact be the vanguard of the era of the empowered consumer, something I had been anticipating with the growth of the Internet and the greater power that consumers enjoyed in every other area of the economy. I knew a great deal about emerging technology and how it would shift the balance of power in the restaurant industry from the kitchen and the boardroom to the private home and the mobile device.

I also knew that the trade media had a profound impact on the restaurant business. There were just a handful of trade magazines and publications dedicated to the restaurant business and no on-line publications of any level of expertise. On the plane ride home I crafted my strategy for what would become FastCasual.com—my trend tracker and news organ for this exciting, disruptive new hybrid restaurant business.

Though I had appointed myself the champion of this new dining model, I knew that trying to get QSRs to appreciate the threat that fast casual posed to their businesses would be difficult—and to get them to admit they could learn something from such a fledgling market segment would be impossible. After all, it was almost impossible to get them to understand the impacts that technological advances such as flat-screen, Windows-powered POS terminals could change their operations for the better. They balked at every chance they had to incorporate such devices into their restaurants. How would I ever get a fast-food giant to admit that the methods of fast casual would likely be its future?

It was at that time that I made the decision to step away from consulting on technology for restaurant companies and become primarily an online publisher. News and information on the Internet were still quite sparse in 1996, and print still ruled the business trade sector of the restaurant industry media. Nation's Restaurant News was the authority on all things fast food, and casual and fine dining, but I suspected they would be as resistant to the idea of fast casual as my audience of executives had been. However, there were a few newer magazines in the niche, and it was these magazines that I approached with the idea of developing a new publishing vertical for the fast-casual segment.

Well, if you remember those halcyon days of online advertising, you know what a struggle I faced in paying the bills. There were not many big online ad budgets and technology pretty much limited us to banners and interstitials, so to make ends meet I decided to continue consulting for major restaurant operations. Only this time I added a new twist to my work. I began to analyze the consumer's mind-set for clues into what was happening in the restaurant industry. I knew that the real magic that I could see developing was not taking place within the corporate offices and restaurant locations of the fast-casual segment itself but instead in the development of the empowered consumer we now refer to in social media circles as the *influencer*.

Understanding the New Consumer

Hot Tip

The key elements of this new era—choice, access, transparency, and the pure desire to get something better faster and for less—were clearly not going away no matter how much the fast-food barons protested. When you added the already fully grown hip, stylish presence of Starbucks to the mix, the consumer was already getting a taste of what it had been missing. I quickly saw that this wasn't just about cost, convenience, or food quality. It was about consumers having allies who would aid them in escaping the tacky plastic orbit of fast food or the overstuffed vibe of fine dining and bringing a new kind of ambience into their daily lives. They wanted choices that reflected their artistic tastes and cultural identity.

This was an amazing development, and the studies I carried out during thousands of hours working inside fast-casual operations all over the country convinced me that the movement was just short of a new work of artistic expression by entrepreneurs, chefs, designers, and technologists. That was why fast food couldn't "get" fast casual: it was about passion first, business second!

For my research, I conducted more than 10,000 interviews with consumers, asking them why they had selected the restaurant they were sitting in. The data was inconsistent, of course, but there was always a common element to their responses: they wanted something better than fast food, and they thought this place was cool. They liked what it said about them that they were eating someplace with a good vibe, a place that felt thoughtful

and creative.

Michael Tchong—analyst, speaker, and founder of Übercool, a groundbreak-

ing marketing-entertainment company, has heavily influenced my thinking in

this area. Michael, a true visionary who is also an incredible entrepreneur

and founder of *MacWEEK*, was one of the first people to recognize that so-

cial media like Facebook and Twitter were doing the same thing that I saw in

the fast-casual model: *social engagement*. His company blends offline immer-

sive, "infotainment events" with targeted online social engagement to create

incredibly powerful marketing and branding experiences.

Michael gets that in this postmodern era, advertising is dying. Traditional

"push" marketing, where the purveyor shoves something new and shiny into

the consumer's face and expects said consumer to buy it, is done. Thanks

to technology like cloud computing and mobile apps, the dynamic is now

two-way and highly collaborative. Consumers want an authentic relationship

with the people who are selling them things, including food. Especially food,

because what's more important than the stuff we put into our bodies?

What Michael calls "social engagement marketing" is the model that's pro-

pelling the insane growth of the fast-casual segment at a time when most

other players in the food service industry are retrenching, cutting headcount,

or suffering. Business that successfully deploy social media are redefining

consumer interaction, he says—a perfect description for what's happening in

fast casual. The smart restaurateurs are using design, technology, and an open

corporate attitude to forge relationships with consumers and turn their feedback into policy. Tweets are impacting menus. Wall updates are determining store locations. Social engagement is the engine of fast casual in a way that it has never been for fast food.

The online magazine *Coolhunting* also profoundly influenced my thinking about social media and fast casual. The website is a stylish, jazzy clearinghouse for information about the latest and newest in everything from personal technology to eco-travel to the latest urban-friendly bike design. As the new reality of restaurants percolated down into my brain, the words of Michael Tchong and the stories and innovations given fresh life on Coolhunting shaped my strategies.

Getting the Word Out

My perception of fast casual as the new dominant paradigm in the restaurant world has been shaped by more than just social networking and technology innovations. As it became clear to me that restaurateurs in this area were reinventing everything about the dining experience, I began looking for insights relevant to the commercial enterprise as a whole. How could fast-casual entrepreneurs change how customers interacted with the space, got their information, and felt about their time in the store?

One of my key influencers in this quest for understanding was Paco Underhill and his seminal book, *Why We Buy*. This became my manual for understanding the psyche of the consumer. Underhill asked why consumers behaved as they did in retail environments and went into stores with a team from his consultancy, Envirosell, to record everything about customer behavior. The patterns he found in the data set the retail world on its ear. He quantified the importance of shopping baskets scattered throughout stores, the impact of contact between employees and shoppers, the importance of the "transition zone" (the area just inside the store's entrance), why men are more likely to buy clothing based on fit than women, and how men are beginning to shop more like their mates (a fact that will be met with howls of protest by men who shudder at being asked to accompany their wives to the mall for any reason other than a movie).

Why We Buy codified for me what I had suspected for years and what so many fast-food barons seemed to refuse to acknowledge: that there are distinct patterns of behavior in how consumers interact with a retail environment and that those patterns can be leveraged to create delight and increase sales. This understanding has helped me advise fast-casual clients on ways to design and redesign their interiors and create visual and tactile stimuli to appeal to the emotions of their target markets, which tend to skew younger and wealthier than the typical fast-food audience.

I also learned a great deal from a technology hero, Robert Scoble. Robert is a Rackspace employee and a troublemaking blogger who loves to stir things up in the tech world with his provocative writings. He is more reliable about keeping his ear to the ground about emerging innovations than anyone else on the Web, and I've gotten the heads-up about social networking applications, mobile platforms, and just about everything else under the sun from him in Silicon Valley and elsewhere.

Robert has diligently documented the evolution of technology and its impact on consumers. He's inspired my own views on the ways that the iPhone and other key tools are affecting the direction of fast-casual marketing and brand development. At the time I started reading his blog daily, the nature of the news media was shifting. It was 2004, and online information, entertainment, and marketing were becoming the new knowledge channels for the restaurant industry, which had somehow always been behind the curve.

I was sure that the movers and shakers of fast casual, who were steeped in the latest tech and very comfortable with it, would be the ones to drag the entire industry kicking and screaming into the era of predictive analytics and the Twitterverse. It had been an uphill battle, being an evangelist for this transformative use of technology and consumer intelligence. In 1999 I approached the National Restaurant Association with the idea that fast casual needed to be watched and its effects on the consumer documented, so that the ways in which it was changing the industry could be applied to benefit the other segments in the restaurant business. I was a decade early to begin to establish an entirely new measurement for the restaurant industry. Fast casual was not ready for the national stage. It needed more innovation and powerful thinking behind it.

The Fast Casual Alliance

The days and months dragged on. I almost gave up on the idea that fast casual would transform the face of the restaurant industry, as I knew it could. It was maddening to be a voice in the wilderness about a subject that I knew could help my industry build a more prosperous future. I was discouraged by the friends I had grown to respect in the fast-food industry, until one day I had a pivotal discussion with the founder of Sonic Drive-In, Troy Smith, at his home in Edmond, Oklahoma.

If you ever met Troy (who left us in 2009), you understand the meaning of service and know that the passion of serving others was his badge of honor. He was a deeply humble man who founded what was at that time the fastest-growing chain of restaurants in the United States. At the time, Sonic had a blistering growth pace and boasted a soaring stock price, fueled by Troy's commitment and amazing executives like Pattye Moore, then president of the company and to this day one of the most innovative people in the industry. (Pattye was one of the first women to break through the glass ceiling of the executive offices of a billion-dollar restaurant brand. She had the gumption, passion, and creativity to take a brand like Sonic to the forefront of the industry. In the 12 years she served with Sonic Corp. as executive vice president, senior vice president, marketing and brand development, vice president of marketing, and president, the company grew from less than $900 million in sales with 1,100 restaurants to over $3 billion in sales and more than 3,000 restaurants. That's extraordinary. Today, Pattye is Chairman of the Board of Red Robin, and they are lucky to have her.)

Troy Smith had retired some years before our fateful meeting, but he often took the time to talk with industry leaders and to give his input on what he thought would help businesses thrive and adapt to the changing times. Still, I never really understood why he agreed to my meeting that day. I was just glad that he did.

Troy was a master at breaking down complex ideas into clear, understandable ideas and actionable plans. As we sat there talking, he mapped out for me the growth curve of McDonald's and why it had happened, and he explained the fall of the venerable A&W brand. He told me that Starbucks would be America's next darling brand because they were doing something nobody else was doing: pushing people to adapt their lifestyles and giving them a place to express those lifestyles.

But what Troy instilled in me on that cold January morning by a roaring fireplace stoked with Oklahoma hickory was that the consumer had *always* been in control of the restaurant business. He explained why he started a *drive-in* as opposed to a drive-thru chain and insisted that the very nature of fast food would someday be utterly changed by technology—because that technology was changing the very nature of *fast*. He predicted that if the fast-food kings didn't do it, others would find a way to bring value to the consumer with convenience and speed.

He was fascinated by my observations about fast casual and grilled me with question after question about operations, consumers, and food. Then he used a term I had not heard before; I'm not sure if he coined it that day, but it has stuck with me ever since. He said, "Do you think that this Internet thing will change the way consumers do everything *in real life*?" (You have to remember this was in the mid 1990s.) After all, Troy had seen such changes occur in his own business, taking it from manual systems and carhops to high-tech communication technology that allowed the Sonic chain to rival the volume of the mighty McDonald's. At the time, average store customer traffic was exceeding two million per year and Sonic was setting records for store openings. Despite all this, Troy knew that the only constant is change. He simply said, "Everything has its time, and I fear we may see the fast-food industry moving to a new place."

That place, he explained to me, was fast casual. I drove away that morning realizing that while vision can sometimes be clouded by circumstances, you either had resolve or didn't. With his quiet wisdom, Troy had set me on my course. He had told me that much of what he'd tried with Sonic—ideas that had made the company such a superstar—had met with the same kind of blind, bull-headed resistance I was encountering. Change always has that effect on people because it makes them feel uncomfortable. But what is life but change? We are always learning, moving, and thinking, and if we can get comfortable with constant change we can learn to master it—to begin to use it as an asset, not a liability.

I realized that I had to keep pushing, because I knew I was right. On that day I decided to split QSRweb.com and FastCasual.com into two separate Web brands. Fast casual was here whether the movers and shakers in fast food wanted to admit it or not—and I was going to be the one who carried the torch. Troy simply had that effect on people; he could make you believe you could climb Mount Everest in Bermuda shorts.

Finally, I realized that if I was going to create a movement, I needed allies. I needed to bring together the best minds in the business to help move fast casual forward at the fast pace I knew it could sustain. In 2004, I had begun to merge my websites with NetWorld Alliance, and began developing the idea for the Fast Casual Alliance and the Fast Casual Executive Summit. The Alliance would be a critical strategic step in helping fast casual make it to the mainstream in the crowded restaurant industry. My strategy was simple: align top leaders in the segment, educate them on what fast casual was and its mission, and create a think tank that could help change the game from the ground up. It was actually a TED ("Technology, Entertainment, and Design" for the uninitiated) Conference I attended in 2001 that actually started me thinking this way. In 1984, TED really launched the idea of bringing together luminaries from multiple disciplines in the same place. I borrowed the concept for the restaurant industry. The FCA, as we began to call the Fast Casual Alliance, began with a small group in Pasadena, California, in 2006. Its mission was simple: help fast casual make it from concept to mainstream market force.

On that fateful day at the Ritz Carlton Huntington Hotel, some of the top visionaries of the food industry came together. Many were and still are leading lights in the restaurant businesses: Louis Basile of Wildflower Bread Company (who would become the first FCA president); Craig Dunaway of Penn Station Subs; Demetris Havadjias of Farmer Boys; Rich Hicks of Better Burger leader Mooyah; Dave Wolfgram of Boudin Bakery; Diana Hovey of Corner Bakery; Alan Hixon, then of Freebirds World Burritos; Matt Andrew, then of Raving Brands; Antonio Swad of Pizza Patron; and Linda Duke of Duke Marketing. Along with this group were industry veterans from Cardtronics, Fishbowl, Micros, Partech, Verifone, and American Express.

Together, we would begin to transform the restaurant industry and bring to light the new ideas, technologies, and philosophies that have made fast casual the leader in value, service, quality—and growth.

Chapter Ten

The Voice of a New Era

I knew that I could not change a $600 billion industry (at the time) by myself. With just one voice, I needed a megaphone—one that would allow me to get my soapbox to the top of the hill and strap a jetpack to it. I began to court a few partners that would allow me to merge my two vertical media outlets, FastCasual.com and QSRweb.com, into a single powerful entity. By 2004, many talks and trips and presentations later, I finally had found my partner: a small, agile, ambitious publisher in Kentucky that was ready to take a risk on the restaurant industry.

They held a single food property, PizzaMarketplace.com, and agreed with me that merging my two properties would set a new tone for the business. More important to me, it would set a new tone for fast casual. Clearly, it was time to do this; some of the top early successes in the category were beginning to spiral into strong growth cycles. I wanted to be the one to chronicle their successes and spread the gospel far and wide in the food industry.

For perspective, let's look at where the fast casual industry was in 2004. At the beginning of that year, Chipotle still operated only 50 stores, with just eight restaurants in Chicago and New York using naturally raised beef. But 2004 marked the onset of the company's extremely ambitious expansion plans; by the end of the year, Chipotle had gained an infusion of cash from McDonald's and grown to more than 400 locations nationwide.

Panera Bread operated 741 company-owned and franchised stores by the end of 2004, compared with a phenomenal 7,500-plus today, and had revenues of $479 million, compared with $1.3 billion in 2010. Meanwhile, at the beginning of 2004, Panda Express had not yet begun operating stand-alone restaurants with drive-thru windows. Today, the chain operates 1,372 locations and is the nation's largest fast-casual Asian food chain. Clearly, fast casual was poised for explosive growth in 2004, and the leaders in the industry were prepared to lead it to new heights and to challenge fast food for dominance.

Style: Goodbye, Plastic Clowns

Numerous factors fueled the growth of these early successes. Among the most important was design style. Before the appearance of fast casual, design was an afterthought in fast food. The ethos was unmistakable: cheap surfaces, garish plastic, hard chairs and tables, and bright lighting, all encouraging patrons to gobble down their food and leave as quickly as possible. Fast-food style was an oxymoron. There was nothing emotionally or sensually pleasing about it.

Starbucks began the change by building stores with a palette of unique, sophisticated qualities designed to appeal to the senses of its customers as urbane aesthetes. The spaces were adorned in signature deep green and chocolate, with café tables, muted lighting, jazz or alternative pop on the sound system, and a corporate attitude that said if customers wanted to linger for hours working on their laptops, they were welcome. The entire package was designed to encourage hanging out.

Chipotle began to mimic Starbucks in the design of its new stores, as did Panera and other major players. Simple and beautiful were the descriptors most often used to explain these new restaurant designs. They employed natural materials, gritty industrial textures, deep colors, comfortable chairs, and an organic sensibility. The contrast between fast casual and fast food was shocking; it was as stark as the difference between a college dormitory and a professionally designed studio apartment. Upon walking into a fast-casual restaurant, the consumer could immediately feel that this was not a fast-food joint, even if they didn't understand the differences in execution or food. That didn't matter. Then as now, most consumers don't really grasp the seismic shift that's taken place in the restaurant industry. They don't need to. They just know that this new class of eateries is classier, more comfortable, more responsive, and serves better food.

It became very clear that places like Chipotle were the hot new places to hang out for lunch. No one wanted to hang out at McDonald's. For most customers, going there was nothing more than a low-cost refueling exercise. Fast casual began using design strategically. Panera Bread's redesign incorporated new tones that were scientifically chosen to affect parts of the consumer's brain associated with pleasure and appetite. Across the country, chains were revamping their lighting and music to mimic that of upscale dining establishments. Fast casual was doing everything it could to separate itself from fast food.

Food Isn't Just Food

The other major factor that drove the boom in fast casual—in those days before the iPhone and Facebook changed everything—was the quality of the food. The days of meaningless refueling with reheated food were over. Customers now expected Mexican from fresh ingredients, bread made from scratch, and burgers crafted with time and care. Troy Smith had known that this change was coming; he understood that the empowered consumer wouldn't be satisfied with a cool interior and a reservation website. The shift was clear to me: from now on, a creative, sustainable, quality-oriented menu would be one of the drivers that would situate fast casual in the sweet spot in American restaurant history.

To put it another way, food has ceased to be just food. In fast casual, it has become the center of an overall experience in the making. Food is critical to many cherished experiences: the first restaurant where you went with your future spouse on your first date, the pizza place where your soccer team would gather after games, the festive Thanksgiving meals that brought together family from all over the country. For the tech-savvy fast-casual customer, reared on local food, farmer's markets, and the Food Network, it's not enough that the food be inexpensive and hot. Taste is no longer the medium of value. The food, just like the design, must suit the customer's self-image: eco-conscious, ultra-fresh, hand-prepared, and uniquely seasoned.

I often explain to fast-casual innovators that food and experience are the key elements that bring people into their restaurants. Remember those 15,000 personal interviews? That's exactly what they said. The consumer is in charge and means what he says.

Celebrity chefs on the Food Network and a hundred food websites not only showed us new culinary delights but told us that yes, such food was available to us—in fact, we *deserved* it. Fast casual responded by specializing. New entrepreneurs and chefs roared onto the scene with vertical power segments like Fresh Mex, Bakery Café, Better Burger, Ethnic and Comfort Food. Focusing on a single type of cuisine gave chefs the ability to zoom in on tiny, incremental areas of quality: fresh vegetables hand-cut in front of ordering customers, artisan bread recipes, variations on beloved classics like grilled cheese or pizza. Food, like design, became a badge of hip, cool, and different.

The Financial Model

The evolution of this new consumer-driven culinary interaction has necessitated the creation of a whole new

Hot Tip

economic model for this industry. In the past the model was complex but actually quite simple:

* Step One: Find great real estate for your flagship store, develop a great concept and consumer brand, make it scalable so you can export the brand to multiple locations or franchisees, and market the hell out of it before you open your first location.

* Step Two: Sell franchises and replicate.

This model may have worked very well during the days of old-school restaurant brand building, but those days are gone. Because consumers are so involved and so pivotal behind the success or failure of restaurant concepts, any financial model simply must factor in the formidable power of the consumer. I have often gone on the record saying there are only a few more 10,000-unit brands left in the restaurant business—but the unflinching truth behind this is that it is the consumer more than any other force that will control whether or not new restaurant concepts rise or fall in this new landscape.

Highly targeted restaurants catering to a tightly focused demographic based on age, ethnicity, or income will begin to become the norm and may even become the preference of this tech-savvy con-sumer. Take Shake Shack and Danny Meyer. Danny and his partners have turned the roadside shake and burger joint into a highly tar-geted concept eatery based on locations in ultra-hip locales such as New York City, Saratoga Springs, New York, Washington, D.C., and Miami, as well as ultra-wealthy enclaves Dubai and Kuwait City. This is attracting a new kind of retro-hip consumer with obscene wealth, attaching an aura of cool and social desirability to the simple, old-fashioned food Shake Shack serves. It's also shattering what was the old goal of two million AVU (Average Unit Volume) by attracting *five million* to some locations. With those economies of scale, you don't need thousands of units and the massive attendant overhead and risk of quality problems that come with that kind of size. You can build an insanely profitable business with hundreds of stores. Small, concentrated, laser-focused, and wildly busy is the new normal in the fast-casual financial world.

The trends show that consumers continue to be extremely choosy about their restaurant brands. That's no surprise; when you have nearly unlimited choices, you'll be selective. The trouble comes when restaurateurs try to build brands on the fast-food model: high volume, questionable quality. That's how McDonald's and Subway became behemoths, but those times are past.

The economic model of the future will be much like what we've seen from brands like Lettuce Entertain You Enterprises. The Chicago-based consortium of restaurant mavens has launched more than 130 restaurants in what you could call "micro-chains," using about 70 concepts to create eateries so targeted that they might be irrelevant outside a surgically chosen, narrow niche. With more than 45 currently active restaurant concepts, the company building brands with high value and unique appeal to highly desirable vertical markets. They are the epitome of what could almost be called "nano branding," branding aimed at an exquisitely small but extremely lucrative niche, such as hipsters in Seattle's Belltown neighborhood.

This is no longer one-size-fits-all marketing, but "what do you want?" brand development. Variety is everything. That's the fuel that fast casual has grown strong on, but too many restaurateurs remain slow on the uptake and continue to model their businesses after the assembly line idea. It's a dead end. Foodlife in Chicago is a perfect example of the future in action: an urban dining center with 14 unique kitchens within a single venue, catering to a vast array of tastes from fresh juices to tacos to barbecue. Tomorrow (and, rapidly, today) is about upscale quality, targeted consumers, and extreme focus, all powered by knowing *everything* about your ideal customer.

The perfect restaurant business will be dynamic, never settling on a single concept or market position. It will be reliable but continually adapting to the new tastes of its nano-market. Successful entrepreneurs will not fall prey to the old financial model but instead create a new model that addresses the needs of the socially savvy consumer. The next great fast-casual concept will create multiple dimensions of the same brand geared toward tiny but fiercely loyal and high-spending market niches, building economics that make our idea of the two million dollar location seem like child's play.

Healthy Is the New Tasty

It's no secret that many Americans are obese. The country is experiencing an unprecedented explosion in both its waistlines and the health care costs related to obesity and a sedentary lifestyle. The Hartman Group report, "How America Eats: The Crucial Role of Food Culture Inside Weight Management," offers a damning look at how Americans perceive the issue of being overweight. In a nutshell, while we are more aware that obesity is a serious problem, we are also more accepting of it and more apt to define our acceptable weight not based on standards given to us by a physician or by the government but by our social network, offline and online.

Food is the enemy in this dysfunctional culture, with consumers citing snacking, eating comfort food, and junk food as the greatest culprits in weight gain. Into this environment comes fast casual, with a golden opportunity to distance itself from the unhealthy, obesity-fostering brand image of fast food that Morgan Spurlock leveraged to such great effect in *Super Size Me*. The timing could not be better. We have an unprecedented economic "reset" in which the rules may have permanently changed. In this environment, high stress and anxiety over money lead to comfort food consumption and weight gain. At the same time, the high cost of health care is forcing more consumers than ever to consider ways to keep themselves healthy and avoid medical needs completely. Fast casual can be the vanguard of this new "healthy is tasty" philosophy.

Healthy eating is the undiscovered country for the restaurant industry—but the real value for consumers is not in purely healthy eating, but in higher-quality food that also happens to be good for us. Though First Lady Michelle Obama has taken up the challenge to get America's youth eating better, the reality is that we just need better education about nutrition and better availability of healthful food in all markets.

What mother concerned about her children's health would shove a fast-food burger into their faces if she could afford and easily access salads, healthy pastas, and fruit smoothies? Consumers want better options, and yet we fall into the "love the one you're with" trap of eating what's at hand more than we would like. I'm as guilty as the next person. Finding food that is quick, healthy, and tasty is still too much work. Chipotle has thrived because in the markets where it is ubiquitous, it owns the ideas of quick/healthy/tasty.

Fast casual may feel like it's leading the healthy eating push, but in reality, consumers still see us more as a total dining experience in which health only plays a small part. Our research shows that while healthy eating is a concern, value tops the list, with quality on its heels. We will always take quality and price, and if the result is also low in fat and sodium and high in vitamins and protein, so much the better.

Food is Hip

Hot Tip

There was a time when someone who raised backyard chickens would have been derided as a hopeless yokel by the skinny jeans and "You've probably never heard of that band, they're too new" crowd. Not anymore. Now urban food producers are rebels, fighting back against The Man's commoditization of food. From fine dining establishments based on foraging to molecular gastronomy based around judicious application of liquid nitrogen. Fresh, organic, locally raised, sustainable food has become as political as any Occupy rally—and therefore, a connection to the hip, opinion-shaping consumers that marketers crave.

Connecting to this crowd is the challenge for today's restaurant and retail brands. Apple is the master at this connection, and the company built its brand on an insane commitment to quality and detail. That is still the answer for any brand, including in the restaurant industry. As we build our businesses, we often take short cuts or think we know better than the consumer. We don't. We can have great ideas, but we had better leaven them with a ferocious curiosity about the consumer and a deep comprehension of what the consumer loves and fears. Few people are visionaries on the level of Steve Jobs. Unless you are, you'd be wise to construct your brand on meaningful consumer interactions.

Focus groups were once the way to do this, but they have run their course. Today's focus groups run 24x7 on Facebook and Twitter. Social media has not only become the intellectual playground for the self-identified hip foodie crowd, but it has also created channels through which we can communicate and get feedback almost instantly. Most companies have anointed journalists and critics as the "tastemakers" in the restaurant business, but smart players know that today, the credibility lies with the consumer— with unedited, real reviews and opinions. The next time you buy a book on Amazon or book a hotel on Hotels.com, look at what data you give the most weight in your decision-making process. I'll bet it's the consumer reviews. When you use Yelp or Oink to choose a place to dine, you do the same thing.

The tech-aware hip crowd is the new tastemaker class, simply because they are connected in so many ways to thousands of others just like them. The ripple effect of that collective opinion is like nothing we have ever experienced in our generation of retail and restaurant business. It can sink or lift a brand in weeks. For this reason, savvy brand leaders today are building relationships with this cohort and immersing themselves in the culture that is driving consumption.

How does the restaurant industry replicate the work that Apple has done in connecting to young, hip consumers willing to spend on the products that strike the right emotional chords? That is the question that every brand executive is asking. The reality is that social media is beginning to link the tastemaker consumer to premium, high-value brands with a variety of new technology and analysis platforms that will serve the needs of the incoming retail and restaurant executive.

Shockingly, the otherwise conservative retailing giant Walmart is setting the pace in this area with its @WalmartLabs play, which I referenced earlier. It's essentially a social media-based search that mines the enormous universe of social media data to customize search results to consumer tastes. Plans are in place to use the information to guide shoppers to products and retailers based on their hobbies and interests, or to help Walmart stores in certain neighborhoods stock more items that fit the tastes of the people tweeting from those localities. That is personalization based on technology, a new era of person-centric search. That organically driven ability to zero in on an individual's tastes and provide solutions will be critical to the development of the restaurants of tomorrow.

Don't Forget the Boomers

Time to contradict myself. While a tight focus on the young, early-adopter hipster crowd will fuel growth in much of the restaurant industry, we cannot and should not ignore the massive Baby Boomer cohort. There are more than 72 million living Boomers in the U.S. and collectively they control about 60% of the nation's wealth even after the Great Recession. Such a massive audience—and the unknowable reality of how it will interact with the food industry—will cause massive shifts as the restaurant business works to cater to these evolving palates and experiential tastes.

When you add the Millennials (people born between 1980 and 2000) to the mix, you have about 167 million consumers who will drive the growth of the restaurant and retail business. The challenge for fast-casual operators—as well as players in every segment of the increasingly specialized restaurant business—will be to come up with offerings that meet the expectations of these two diverse groups. Apple has managed to do it quite well: walk into an Apple store and you see a wide range of consumers, each with its own segment of products, each interacting with sales staff in a different manner. Dining tastes may vary, but is it possible to design the experience so that it creates delight ("enchantment" to go back to Guy Kawasaki) in both Millennials and Boomers? Can restaurateurs build in sufficient customization to allow both groups to have as much or as little machine or human interaction as they desire?

The short answer is yes. There is a real opportunity for well-developed brands to crack this code. The menu will have to break some molds, and the interaction models will need to be radically different from what most diners experience, but this is possible. One thing that fast-casual entrepreneurs can count on is that their customer demographics are not only friendly to business experimentation but actively *encourage* it. Education, exploration, and innovation will define the evolution of restaurant brands. Those who explore new tastes and engagement strategies, and employ cutting-edge technology and challenge preconceptions about the very culture of service, will dominate in the future.

Here Comes the Internet

Once upon a time, there were newspaper food criticism columns, and we all devoured them like they were gourmet meals. The critics who wrote them were like the Anton Ego character in the film *Ratatouille*, powerful, feared, and respected. That was then, and for better or worse, this is now.

Bloggers have taken over the food writing scene. There are an estimated 212,000 food bloggers in the United States, Europe, South America, and China. While that means that a lot of rank amateurs are writing about food, it also means a staggering range of opportunities exists to reach out to food consumers and gain brand exposure.

Before the age of the blogger, The Food Network was the main game changer for chefs and restaurants. Its programming could change the fortunes of a brand overnight. But with more than 200 million foodies visiting culinary blogs every day, it's safe to say that the balance of power has changed. Blog readership dwarfs Food Network viewership. Sure, the audience is splintered, but that's the case with media in general; just check the channel lineup on your satellite dish network. The pertinent fact is that there is a vast amount of content coming from the food blog ecosystem—most of which is pretty good—and collectively it is changing the way consumers get information about new restaurants, find their favorites, and educate themselves about chefs, cuisines, preparation methods, and technologies.

Yelp is the king of recommendation networks, but as in many things, Google is looming. The search giant plans acquisitions in the food space, which means we could see the biggest player of all take a strong position in curating reviews for the food industry. The coming battle will be epic and will only benefit restaurateurs as Yelp, Google, and many other players compete to see who can be more hyper-local and who can come up with cooler, more useful features. Over time, whatever technology comes from this will change how consumers navigate the world of dining as surely as smart phones and iPads have redefined consumer choice today.

Perhaps more than in any other space of consumer activity (health care might be a match), opinion will be the killer app that drives the success of fast-casual brands with the smarts to leverage the explosion in mobile tech, video, and social networks. From the FastFood app to "food porn" blog networks like Tastespotting.com and Thedailyblender.com, the technologies and business models that most successfully connect hungry consumers with the subjective, experience-shaped opinions of diners, critics, chefs, artisan food makers, and farmers will see the greatest benefit to their brands and bottom lines. When it comes to food, we want the "I was there, and..." view. Technology may help us make reservations, but we want to know what it tasted like and how the service was.

Hot Tip

The Social Consumer

Bringing all this together—mobile tech, personal opinion, and the cultural impact of foodies and food—will be social media. That's the heart of the Chipotle Effect. Fast casual has been on the forefront of using social media as a branding tool with concepts like Chipotle, Panera, Five Guys Burgers, Pei Wei, Firehouse Subs, Which Wich, Wing Stop, and more.

Because of these fresh concepts, we also met a new consumer who is more engaged with Facebook, Twitter, Flickr, LinkedIn, and YouTube. Combine this with the mainstream integration of mobile Internet for everything from banking to travel booking and we have a consumer who has grown up much faster that the food brands that cater to him.

Imagine a future where the restaurant chain with the largest marketing budget doesn't automatically claim the largest market share. Now stop imagining. That time is here. Social media, together with an understanding of everything else I have written about in this chapter, will entail greater levels of connection and interaction with this empowered breed of consumer. The brands with the best grasp of the technology and the most talented, innovative people will win.

Don't believe it? Witness the 2011 Chadwick Martin Bailey Report "10 Quick Facts You Should Know About Consumer Behavior on Twitter." According to this survey of 1,491 online consumers, 79% of Twitter users follow fewer than ten brands, and do so in order to be "in the know" and get exclusive offers and information—making them a choosy and loyal group. Twitter users are interacting with followed brands more as time passes, and those who follow brands rarely un-follow them. Finally, 60% said they are likely to recommend a brand to someone else after following it.

In other words, Twitter users are power consumers: loyal, engaged, and talkative. And according to this study, Twitter may be early in its growth cycle, meaning the reach of key influencers on the network will only expand. What smart fast-casual entrepreneur wouldn't build a strategy designed to turn Twitter into a major brand building and revenue-producing channel? Forget TV ads. Forget event sponsorships. Social media is leveling the playing field and everyone is playing.

The Great Google Era

Finally, there is Google, the soundtrack that plays in the background of every technology achievement of the past ten years. As Apple dominates the hardware world, Google dominates the Web or the cloud as we like to call it these days —and will continue to do so in ways that we cannot possibly imagine. Whenever I or anyone I know becomes too smug about the advances we enjoy today, I like to pull out a quote from German scientist Georg Christoph Lichtenberg, which says, "Perhaps, in time, the so called dark ages may be the ones we live in today."

Indeed. If that is to be so, it will be Google that ushers in a new age of technological innovation in software, services, search, information utility, robotics, space travel—the list is endless. That quote always reminds me that the landscape is changing beneath our feet. Search is changing radically, social is shifting culture, politics, and most of all the consumer mind-set, and that change will impact the restaurant industry in a life-or-death manner. In the coming years, search will adapt and introduce innovations that will shape how consumers interact with everything in their worlds.

Everything you undertake as a businessperson over the next five years must take into account mobile, search, and social technology before you consider *any other facet* of how you market to, interact with, or profit from your customers. Often, the conversation stops at marketing, but search and the convergence of social, mobile, and local is much more. We are constructing businesses even as our teams, locations, cultures, menus, suppliers, and customers shift at a new speed of change— "business is no longer business as usual." Some entrepreneurs will be equipped to deal with this fluid world in which the rules change weekly. Others will not.

Search-based marketing could not save the casual dining business. This is not about marketing. The current generations are too smart for marketing. They demand transparency, authenticity, and customization. The great players are already shifting and building in new directions. They know that where Google goes, so goes technology.

Is the future hyper-local? Google Places? There is a holy grail of search and social media, and it might be where Google, Twitter, and Facebook collide. Or perhaps one will simply challenge the others with some unforeseeable innovation.

Chapter Eleven

What is the Chipotle Effect?

As I have discussed here, the evolution of the fast-casual business is a certainty. The direction of that evolution is not. As the leaders of that segment, you as an individual and we as a collective need to be intimately in touch with the consumer and the technologies available to better serve the consumer. While the consumer love affair with fast casual is on a roll and the future looks extremely bright, love affairs have a habit of fading into recrimination and rejection when one partner in the relationship does not attend to the needs of the other.

What is certain is that the future will look nothing like the present. Just as the people who carried Motorola's RAZR cell phone in the 1990s could never have predicted the smartphones of today, we cannot imagine the shape that dining will take in the 2020s or 2030s. But we can try. Here are some of my predictions about trends to come in fast casual and elsewhere.

First, two new segments are already starting to emerge and somewhat eclipse fast casual. The first is what I call *Convenience Gourmet*. The second I have labeled *Gourmet Casual*. Now, what need do these new segments fill? Well, let's look at the new economic reality. By all accounts, the United States and possibly the world are in a prolonged period of economic slowness. In five to ten years, will the average person want to sit down for a three-hour meal and pay the tab? Probably not. However, we will still crave a temporary retreat where we can slow things down a bit and enjoy our food. Hence these two new but rising segments.

Let's break them down:

Hot Tip

* **Gourmet Fast Food**—This will replace fast food and might even step in to overshadow fast casual, but the focus will be on speed and high quality at a great price. Wait a second, isn't that what fast casual does already? Maybe, but Convenience Gourmet will require us to incorporate new drive-thru technology and much faster delivery times to appease the masses who will still want fast-food speed. McDonald's

is probably closer to this than any current fast-casual operators, but that was the sacrifice that fast casual chose to make: creating an experience for the consumer that was focused on quality and values, not speed. In the past that did not hurt fast-casual dining, since speed at the expense of everything else was the hallmark of the fast-food brands that so many consumers were abandoning. But some fast casuals are becoming more like casual dining establishments, so the "fast" part of the category is weakening. In the future, this will not be the case. Consumers will demand both excellent quality and in-car convenience.

Freshii, the Canadian-run fast-casual franchise with 35 locations in four countries, is an example of Convenience Gourmet in its nascent form. I like to call this "fast forward cuisine" that is grab-and-go friendly while retaining a focus on quality and freshness. At Freshii, customers choose from a selection of chef-designed items or create their own customized salads, wraps, bowls, or soups from a selection of more than 70 fresh ingredients and dressings. The customer writes his or her concoction on a paper receipt (there's room there for innovation; what about a touch screen?) and pays, and the order is then "designed" with the desired toppings and dressings.

This is convenience, variety, and freshness at their zenith. Protein Bar in Chicago (which homes in on low-fat, high-fiber, high-protein foods) and The Mixx in Kansas City offer the same type of highly customizable experiences for busy professionals focused on health and value. Think of it as food artistry for people who want choice but need good food fast.

* **Upscale Fast Casual**—We currently have hundreds of thousands of casual dining restaurant locations competing for the consumer dollar. Add to that the smaller category of Fine Dining and the evolution of high-end fast casual and you get what should be the heart of the restaurant industry's growth for the better part of a decade.
For an example of this hybrid approach, let's take a look at Lime Fresh Mexican Grill in Miami. This is a fast-casual concept that prides itself on being like Chipotle, but just a little bit classier. At Lime Fresh, you'll find a greeter at the door, people running your food to you at your table and even checking back to make sure everything's OK. It's fast casual plus limited table service.
Time for food delivery in a busy lunch rush: eight to twelve minutes. That's fast, but not fast-food fast. However, this is a segment still feel-

ing out what the consumer wants. The point is that the subtle shad-ings of this segment—fast casual only different—are already begin-ning to splinter into higher-quality service on one side and speed on the other.

Don't get me wrong; speed will still be important. The differ-ence is that the restaurant industry of the future will feature play-ers in about six or seven distinct verticals—Fast Food, Fast Casual, QSR, Convenience Gourmet, Gourmet Casual, Casual Dining, and Fine Dining, for now—that will give the consumer nearly unlimited choice while possibly requiring a scorecard or rating service to ex-plain which is which. What's more, there will also be express lanes, drive-thrus, mobile ordering for pickup, and onsite ordering options. Companies that provide ways that I can slow my life down after I've dealt with my overflowing email inbox, my Facebook updates, and my Twitter streams will be my new favorites, and I suspect it will be the same for millions of others. It will be these businesses that have a unique place in the future of the restaurant industry.

I haven't gone completely off the deep end; fine dining and fast food will still have their devotees. But the bulk of food consump-tion will move to the middle. I'm used to being the prophet crying in the wilderness; in 1996, most people told me that fast casual would never exist. When I started publishing FastCasual.com and QSRweb.com, some people insisted that the Internet was just a fad. Magazines and newspapers would be around forever, so why would I ever want to create a website for news and information about the restaurant industry? Well, 12 years later, every restaurant industry trade publication has an online presence. The future is hard to predict but always changing.

As my mentor Troy Smith said, "Customers will always be in control of our business. It's those who think they can control the customer that will fail." This quote appears almost verbatim on every social media presentation I see today, from Wall Street to Silicon Valley. The landscape has not really shifted that much; we just happen to know what customers really want now because they have the tools to tell us. Ask yourself: had you been in the forefront of fast casual, could you have been the Chipotle or the Panera of the industry? Could you have been Starbucks? Do you have that kind of vision? People who think differently help us all think differently. Thinking differently spawns creativity and innovation. I challenge you to think like a disrupter—to do it with passion, not recklessness. A real innovator knows the difference.

The Evolution of the Chipotle Effect

Our business will evolve. That much is certain. It's been evolving since the first McDonald's opened its doors. What's changed is the speed of that adaptation and change. It's increased a hundredfold. So while the consumer love affair with fast casual is at a peak and the future looks extremely bright, it's impossible to predict where the evolutionary process will take us. The increasing power of the Web and social media will have a profound impact on the restaurant business over the next two decades. For those who adapt well, the impact will be unimaginably fast growth and profitability. For those who resist, the effects will be devastating.

The next Chipotle Effect is out there right now, probably taking shape in the worlds of mobile media, information search, or a new iteration of the social network. Figuring out the nature of this next leap forward for fast casual is the Holy Grail of this industry. Fast casual has forever changed the landscape of the American restaurant industry in a way that has given us the chance to connect meaningfully to the new consumer in ways that fast food never could. Only through foresight will we leverage this opportunity.

The opportunity is one that I continue to see in my dreams, one that positions the restaurant business with the new age consumer in a way that that is revolutionary. We connect to more people on a daily basis than any other business sector on the planet, and it is our opportunity to win or lose. Fast casual will have a global impact on leading nations that embrace these connected consumers. The future of what we are about to see in the restaurant industry will take some major resolve to change, one thing the restaurant industry does not do well. This is where the innovators of fast casual, I believe, will make the difference, but only a select few will get it. There are only so many visionaries like Steve Ells and Howard Schultz out there. We must change now; the consumer is blazing past us on a rocket ship loaded with iPhones, tablets, and social networks, and the future of this business is dependent on how we connect with them at this critical time.

The combination of quality, speed, access, and customer experience is changing almost every sector of consumer activity, from banking to health care. We all benefit from the work of the innovators who have revolutionized the means for connecting with and servicing the consumer. There will be many such players in the fast-casual segment. Some will copy what's already being done and confuse the consumer. But the real Chipotle Effect—that revolutionary means of tapping in to what the consumer cares about and loves—cannot be copied. It's about personal insight and instinct as much as technology and consumer science.

Hot Tip

Building the Next Chipotle Effect

The person or persons who discover the next Chipotle Effect will possess one critical quality: *curiosity*. Best-selling marketing writer Seth Godin speaks passionately about the virtues of curiosity; he holds that while fundamentalists look to see what matches their belief systems before exploring, the curious go exploring and decide if they want to accept what they find. Curiosity might have killed the cat, but it's the first principle behind the kind of restless, open-minded investigation that leads to the toppling of conventional wisdom and the creation of innovative business models.

Witness Godin's take on the dysfunctional book publishing business model. In a speech for the Independent Book Publishers, he pointed out that the modern publishing model is irretrievably broken, as is the record industry, which is all but dead thanks to downloadable music files. In this speech, Godin rightly asserts that without curiosity, the publishing business has become obsolete because publishers have approached new technologies with fear and not curiosity.

"The top of the ecosystem is moving," he said in his speech. The book business's best customers are using electronic media, eliminating manufacturing, traditional promotion, and other crucial aspects of the publishing business model. These are beneficial changes, yet publishers have been dangerously slow to adapt to these changes or realize that they need to empower these shifts rather than resist them. If we are not curious and adaptive, we fight back against change until it runs over us.

Being curious is the beginning of the answer to every problem in our industry. With the right mindset, we can move from confronting realities that we thought we never would to accepting new truths that many people still think are a waste of time. Had I not been curious, fast casual may have never been defined, curated, or accepted by the masses. My curiosity was part of what motivated the tribe of people leading these brands to think outside the box and step into to the unknown without knowing if there was a reward. As Godin says, our role will be to lead, connect a tribe, and create a movement. Curiosity will lead the next evolution of our business.

As author and innovation guru Linda Bernardi says in her book *Provoke*, disrupting the present is what creates the innovation of the future. We have to be ready to tear down what's being done today in order to create what will produce even greater success tomorrow.

Welcome to the Food (Social) Network

Hot Tip

In all, the restaurant business is in position for a complete makeover over in the next five years. This shift will merge a new breed of operators with stunningly elegant communications, research, and marketing technology, and will parallel the complete makeover of the global consumer that's occurring today.

Brian Solis's new book, *The End of Business As Usual*, captures the essence of this edge-of-the-chasm era beautifully. In this book, Solis, principal at the Altimeter Group, a research-based advisory firm, says that the newly minted and global power of consumers to share their experiences and opinions with each other without the slightest filtration by any business intermediary has changed the game forever. In this new world, shared experiences are redefining brands and forcing operators of all kinds of businesses to bring their A-games in order to win the trust and loyalty of people who have, essentially, unlimited choice and zero tolerance for bullshit.

As Solis writes, the consumer is now "steering the experience." For the restaurant business, this is a challenging but hopeful shift. After all, we have been refining the idea of hospitality for 100 years. Consumers understand what we do. We get them for 30 or 60 minutes, not for the six minutes it takes to walk into a grocery store, grab a few items, and leave. We have the ability to guide the conversation—and even better, to move consumers to choose us more often. The future will be built from the consumer's perspective, not the entrepreneur's. The fast-casual players who are able to peer out from behind the consumer's eyes to create a unique, authentic, and enchanting experience are the ones who will own the next evolution of our business.

Savvy fast-casual businesses will be able to use the growing consumer influence to their advantage. We have always known as much as we can about our customers, but the difference is that in the new age of social business, the influencer is not the same target as in the past. Today, influencers are moving targets. They can build massive audiences and drive trends through viral videos or hot tweets. In the past, an influencer was commonly a local business leader, celebrity, sports figure, or authority figure. Now, it's the person who best captures the underlying thoughts and emotions of the masses in a blog post or 140 characters. That's the person we're after—and everybody else is after him or her, too.

Connection with these key consumers will not be via traditional marketing channels but via so-called "touchpoints." Over the coming years, we will reinvent the way we interface with our top customers. This gives fast casual the chance to do something really special: sculpt experiences and build a truly unique experience memory bank for consumers—who now have the ability to share those memories with hundreds, thousands, or even millions. How will these new methods reshape our business? Here are some likely outcomes:

 = 3.0

Leadership 3.0

- Leadership 3.0 development to redefine how they lead the new consumer and the new workforce
- New online and in-store environments
- Turning marketing teams into Engagement teams assembled from marketing, HR, and operations
- Companies with Chief Digital Media and Chief Content Officers
- Digital command centers tracking all things brand and segment or interest area related

- Social tactic training for all new hires, both management and frontline
- Frontline people become virtuosos in the use of tablet computers for everything from instant online interaction to order fulfillment to guest entertainment
- New storytelling briefs from suppliers
- Company websites run on Content Management Systems to power rich, social media in written, audio, and video form
- Use of social media in every aspect of the business, from hiring to marketing

Yes, it's the end of the world as we know it, and the opportunity to change the way people eat is right in front of us.

Mobile Food: Redefining "To Go"

Another trend that we will draw from in redefining fast casual is the absolutely incredible boom in street food via upscale food trucks and mobile pop-up restaurants. These may be a fad, but in some cities, they are rewriting the rules on local, flexible, tech-friendly dining. We're way beyond taco trucks, folks.

We should watch "mobile food" very closely—not because we need to reorganize our business around trucks and roadside stands, but because this trend reflects important consumer behavior. As I have stated, mobile food is exploding because consumers are seeking something that the larger market has left unattended: local authenticity, a sense of real food prepared by a chef who grew up in the area and not focus grouped to a fare-thee-well. As business engineers we can learn from this. It's incumbent upon us to identify the market deficiency that mobile street food is meeting and change some of our models to address the consumer need that this segment is clearly satisfying. Consumer *actions* are temporary, but consumer *behavior* is long-lasting and trendsetting in a way that often changes daily habits.

Lars Perner, Ph.D., assistant professor of clinical marketing at the Marshall School of Business at the University of Southern California, has commented on this reality on his website:

Social factors...influence what the consumers buy—often, consumers seek to imitate others whom they admire, and may buy the same brands. The social environment can include both the mainstream culture (e.g., Americans are more likely to have corn flakes or ham and eggs for

breakfast than to have rice, which is preferred in many Asian countries)
and a subculture (e.g., rap music often appeals to a segment within the
population that seeks to distinguish itself from the mainstream popula-
tion). Thus, sneaker manufacturers are eager to have their products
worn by admired athletes. Finally, consumer behavior is influenced by
learning—you try a hamburger and learn that it satisfies your hunger
and tastes good, and the next time you are hungry, you may consider
another hamburger.

As entrepreneurs, we must pay close attention to those social
trends that influence what is acceptable and even approved by the
social fabric. A few years ago, it was not acceptable to take a date
to a food truck; now it's not only acceptable but *de rigeur*. The social
fabric has made it so, and via social networks fast-casual restaurateurs have an excellent tool to monitor those warps and redirects in
the social conversation—if we're paying attention. We'd better be.

The Future of Vending

Even as fast casual and unforeseeable types of dining rise to
prominence in the future, new food packaging and creative culinary

elements will make it into the vending machines and convenience stores of the future. The availability of quality food to fill my belly will come from advanced new vending technology and food manufacturing, ranging from protein concoctions to burger vending machines that deliver In 'N' Out-like quality.

Vending technology may not be as sexy as mobile phone technology, but it is far more practical and surprisingly advanced. The latest vending technology sells juicy hamburgers and slider-style hot dogs that don't resemble the scary "death dogs" that for years have been the subject of humor on shows like *The Simpsons*. There are machines that custom-assemble and mix your chosen healthy drink (acai or pomegranate, for example) in a convenient pouch. There are vending machines that custom-brew and dispense gourmet coffee, and which will give you your food free in return for watching an advertisement. The Let's Pizza machine actually makes dough and cooks your personal pizza fresh in three minutes.

In Australia, Food Cube machines store frozen potatoes, fry them in oil in less than two minutes and serve them with dipping sauce and a napkin. The MooBella machine blends, aerates, and freezes 96 different flavors of ice cream on demand, with an interactive touch screen that lets you blend your own final product, complete with mix-in goodies. Finally, Kraft Foods, Crane Merchandising Systems, Samsung, and Digitas have partnered to create what could be called the iVend: a state-of-the-art vending computer with a 46-inch Samsung LCD touch-screen panel that displays available items, gives customers a 360-degree view, and provides ingredient and nutritional information.

We're a long, long way from those old candy bar machines with the "pull here" knobs. Today's vending technology uses biometric readers to confirm the age of certain customers based on facial wrinkles and delivers hot, freshly cooked cuisine that, while it may not approach the quality or freshness of a meal from a fast-casual dining room, far surpasses the standards of those forlorn convenience store hot dog carousels. For the consumer, this means one thing: more choice. Companies in the $30 billion U.S. vending industry are working hard to provide even more low-cost options to time-crunched, economically challenged consumers. That can only raise the bar for all fast-food and fast-casual businesspeople. You're not the only cheap, tasty game in town anymore.

Consumer Trend Maps

Managing this new array of tools and demands can be overwhelming. That's why I've created a tool that I call the Consumer Trend MapSM. Over the past couple of years at my company, DigitalCoCo.com, we have been developing a technology and an algorithm that tracks social behavior and actions. Social media consumers leave small trails of insight into their behavior that I call "social maps." These maps, along with other actionable data, are the raw materials of the next phase of innovation in fast casual. They will be the fuel for the next Chipotle Effect.

This is why @WalmartLabs is putting millions into a social consumer monitoring technology that derives social shopping habits. It's why Starbucks is making plans to mine consumer social data in a huge way—a natural fit when you scan their massive social media reach, approaching 30 million consumers in 2011. I predict that by 2015 they will hit 60 million! Imagine the trends and influence the Starbucks brand could shape with the right approach.

So how do you build a "Consumer Trend Map"? First, you must understand what the consumer needs and wants. Social media has provided that better than any research system we have ever deployed, so pay attention to the data.

There are two types of trend-directing consumers. The first is the "Super Influencer," who influences markets from the very edge of new trends. This consumer sees and interacts more with new ideas and is the earliest of early adopters. The second is the "Impact Consumer or Secondary Influencer."

This consumer is most important of all because they regularly communicate their behaviors to their entire social media circle, becoming influencers. However, the Impact Consumer takes his cues from the Super Influencer and will rarely make a move without the implied approval of this resident of the cutting edge, so you must account for and appeal to both in your marketing.

1. **Identify the influencers** who define your business or brand.

2. **Determine the key behavioral trends** of the influencers. For example, do they tend to only try new restaurant brands if given a discount coupon?

3. **Study the Impact** Consumers who are affected by the Influencers.

4. **Identify the brands and business** that both groups gravitate toward.

5. **Look for the similarities** in their behavior toward those brands.

6. **Identify the brand activities** or unique qualities that drive that behavior.

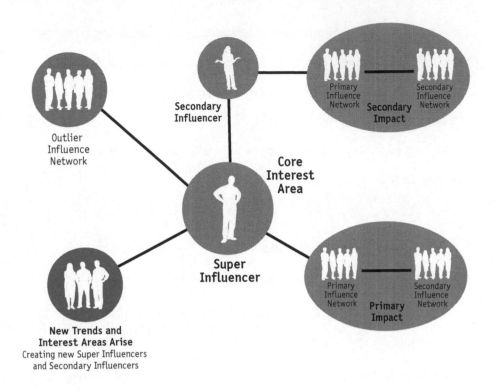

**Outlier
Influence
Network**

Secondary
Influencer

Primary
Influence
Network

Secondary
Influence
Network

**Secondary
Impact**

**Core
Interest
Area**

**Super
Influencer**

Primary
Influence
Network

Secondary
Influence
Network

**Primary
Impact**

**New Trends and
Interest Areas Arise**
Creating new Super Influencers
and Secondary Influencers

With this data you will be able to identify the characteristics of the brands that motivate your key consumers' behavior, which will allow you to begin developing your own business strategies for emulating those successful brands.

Crowdsourcing and Chaos Theory

But individual consumers are not the only path to success. "Crowdsourcing" has become a powerful business model unto itself. Innovators like Kickstarter.com and Designcrowd.com are just the vanguard of business models that tap the genius and wisdom of crowds. Kickstarter, for example, has revolutionized creative production for writers, artists, filmmakers, musicians, and more by introducing what could be called "group patronage." Via this website, potential patrons review carefully selected creative arts and communication projects. When they find something that speaks to them personally, they can choose to invest in it. When the artist reaches a set fundraising goal, the money is transferred and the project can begin. It's extraordinary.

Crowdsourcing of this type has the potential to utterly disrupt the feedback channels of the entire restaurant industry. Most brands listen to customers through feedback systems and focus groups that are slow and highly controlled. That is an obsolete model. Crowds feed off interaction. They can be finicky and unpredictable, but in reality that is exactly what you want. The controlled chaos of an unfettered group feedback channel can produce synergistic results akin to the so-called "butterfly effect," in which a small change at one point in a nonlinear system can result in massive differences down the line in that system's evolution, such as a hurricane's formation being affected by whether or not a distant butterfly had flapped its wings weeks before.

Crowdsourcing can take a simple idea in a huge variety of directions. I have begun to build on the idea of crowdsourced brand development. Most companies won't take the risk of crowdsourcing, but this is one of the most powerful tools you can use to develop an advantage over your competitors. Idea mills and brain trusts are great, but something magical happens when you place people from all walks of life and cultural backgrounds into a single ecosystem and watch what happens. That's the beauty of Facebook and Twitter: they are crowdsourcing mechanisms let run free.

What can you do to take advantage of this resource? First, change your thinking on customer interaction. Empower it rather than restricting it. Rule #1 in social media is, "They will do it any-way." Your task is to provide consumers with a fresh, robust, and inviting environment that will entice them to shape your business through crowdsourced feedback: text, photos, video, and voice. That's unfiltered, raw data that will reveal new consumer behaviors that can lead to the Next Big Idea. Check out DigitalCoCo.com to explore this in greater detail.

How Fast Food Nation Became Fast Casual Nation

Hot Tip

The consumer shift behind all this tremendous change

is happening, driven by many factors: the economy, technology, the Food Network, a backlash against corporate control of our food supply, the availability of a vast and growing selection of information on every restaurant in existence, and more. The fact remains that our consumer landscape has permanently changed. Let's look at each of these factors:

* **The economy**—With unemployment holding steady at around a dismal 9% (and the underemployment rate, including those who have given up looking for work, thought to be at an ever more horrific 16%), consumers have been forced to downgrade from casual dining and even from fast casual in some cases. Chipotle was poised to meet new need for increased value while launching its social media outreach to let consumers know that quality, speed, and experience could be had at a lower price point without spending money on a tip. That is the new normal. No matter what happens in the economy, this consumer is never going back to the days of overspending for food and an experience, because they have found an undiscovered segment of the restaurant industry that will transform itself to suit them.

* **The Food Network**—We're all foodies now, thanks to this clearinghouse of culinary information. This has immediate impact on fast food; you can see the responses from behemoths like McDonald's and its McCafe success. Expect other fast food giants to look at new models of serving better quality food with an improved experience. Wendy's

is an early player in this area, as may Burger King and Sonic be, as fast food steps up to meet fast casual.

* **Technology**—Social media is in its infancy. Mobile technology is starting its climb to dominate our lives. The Internet is booming as never before. Because of all this data and utility, consumers are both accepting things we assumed just a decade ago that they never would, and driving innovations by applying relentless pressure to adapt or die. Mark 2010 as the Year of the Fast Casual Consumer, because that's when they took over our business.

* **Local, organic, and authentic**—Forces like Occupy Wall Street are only the latest stage in a long-evolving backlash against factory farms, corporate chain restaurants, engineered food, and canned marketing. Consumers today want local, real, and genuine.

Global Impact

Hot Tip

Ours is becoming a global industry, and the global impact of the Chipotle Effect is already being felt in the social ecosystem that continues to show us new ways to build our businesses. Europe is an ever-expanding culinary market and an up-and-coming consumer trend hotbed, and the growth of fast casual in this part of the world is already under way. The European economic crisis—at this writing, Greece's likely default and massive debt and Italy's deficits threatening to spread to the French economy—could hinder growth temporarily, but as this impacts the Continent's long-established fine dining scene, fast casual will be well positioned to capture market share.

China is perhaps the growth market for fast casual that has the most titanic potential. First is the raw fact that the Chinese economy is an engine that won't quit, with a growth rate of more than 9% a year even after a recent slight slowdown. This new prosperity inevitably leads to consumers demanding more choice, and the Chinese as a people want to choose from among American brands. The Chinese have already embraced Starbucks, Apple and Nike and are poised to devour many more top American brands perceived to be of high quality. Without question, this creates opportunities for fast-casual brands to expand to this enormous market—experiential brands like what fast casual has developed over the past decade. Fast food's time has come and gone in the Chinese market. Brands that can deliver an American experience with quality, speed, and value will enjoy wild success.

What is America's Next Great Restaurant?

Hot Tip

The future of how consumers interact with brands is dynamic and only beginning to take shape. Something special is under way, a potential Golden Age of restaurants and retail. We can look forward to some amazing innovations. Technology will play a significant role in the future of this business with social media, new evolutions in HR, and a dramatic restructuring of corporation operations to address what will be America's Next Great Restaurant business.

NBC is already on the bandwagon, aware that the nation's food obsession can only grow. Its reality one-season reality show, "America's Next Great Restaurant," pitted competitors against one another to create the best concept restaurant—in this case, a soul food eatery called Soul Daddy. Though the show was cancelled after its single season, there will undoubtedly be others like it. We are fascinated by food and those who bring it to us, and I don't see that changing. If anything, it is accelerating.

Our biggest challenge is leveraging the many opportunities we have right now. Many believe that a new breed of entrepreneurs will set the pace for the next two decades in fast casual, but I feel that our current industry leaders, who have grown up in the technology era and have the experience and practical knowhow, will be the ones to discover and develop the hot new concepts.

I predict that we will see a market correction in fast casual in 2013. Many upstart brands will either fail or be acquired, simply because they were not prepared for strategic growth. We are in a precarious position: trying to drive revenue growth while working to position our businesses as brands that consumers can connect to and trust. It's a rough balancing act.

The next great American restaurant business will rise from a mix of sales growth and brilliant branding using technology. Brand impact is massively different than just a decade ago. Remember the viral online Old Spice campaign that responded to consumer tweets? That was a sharp, daring campaign that revitalized a tired brand with creative fire and genius social media use. By displaying an insane 205 short videos over a three-day period based on real-time consumer suggestions, the Old Spice channel became the most watched YouTube channel ever. It got more than 100 million views and gained the brand 80,000 Twitter followers in two days. In four weeks, Old Spice sales jumped 106%.

That's a model that fast casual does well, and the restaurants of tomorrow will do it even better. Targeting the socially networked, tech-aware consumer will take us in whole new directions as the "consumer science" of our business becomes clear. Data and analytics will drive brands and sales strategies and it will be the companies that take consumer science seriously that will become the next Chipotles.

Gone are the days when we could promote what we want and throw a budget into a marketing campaign without understanding the consumer audience. Today, the consumer audience is not just frequenting our business—the consumer is *part of our business*. This is not just about Facebook, Twitter, Google, Yelp and YouTube. It's about a fundamental reorientation the consumer's role as it relates to businesses. It will take amazing leaders to translate this reality shift into growth—to take a $750 billion industry to one trillion dollars by 2020.

What's the formula for the next Great American Restaurant? It will be easy to see, but not so easy to execute:

Mastering the Chipotle Effect

Innovation + Idea ÷ Leadership ability × consumer science understanding √

Compounded by social and digital media ÷ technology deployment × New breed of employee =

New consumer love affair with brand

It's up to you to get us there.

Chipotle Effect
Definition

The Chipotle Effect is the process that allows a small organization armed with a clear vision of product and purpose to match the amazing demand and growth of the social consumer. Most businesses can't—they are just too slow. This effect is often compared to what Apple did to the entertainment and mobile industries and is about to do to the television business.

Speed, vision, and seeing beneath the surface of society is the key to replicating what Chipotle Mexican Grill has accomplished in the restaurant business.

"It does not take sharp eyes to see the sun and the moon, nor does it take sharp ears to hear the thunderclap. Wisdom is not obvious. You must see the subtle and notice the hidden to be victorious."

Sun Tzu, The Art of War

Index

C

D

N

S

U

V

The Chipotle Effect

Dedicated to my Mother. Thank you for instilling the
passion for serving others and helping me believe
that anything is possible.

I miss you.

For Speaking Arrangements contact the Author at

www.chipotleeffect.com

on Twitter @chipotleeffect

All images, maps and processes are

designed by the Author

Paul Barron.

Mastering the Chipotle Effect

Innovation + Idea + Leadership ability × consumer science understanding √

Compounded by social and digital media + technology deployment × New breed of employee =

New consumer love affair with brand

Super Influencers represent
the leading targets for
brands of the future

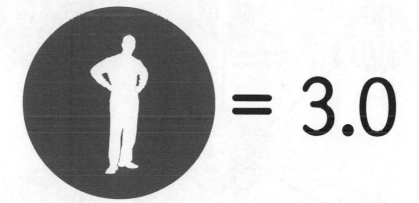

Leadership 3.0

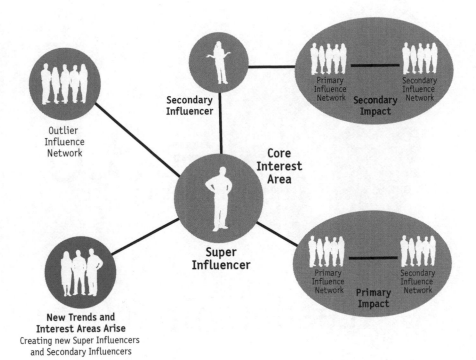

Secondary
Influencer

Outlier
Influence
Network

Primary
Influence
Network

Secondary
Influence
Network

**Secondary
Impact**

Core
Interest
Area

Super
Influencer

Primary
Influence
Network

Secondary
Influence
Network

**Primary
Impact**

**New Trends and
Interest Areas Arise**
Creating new Super Influencers
and Secondary Influencers

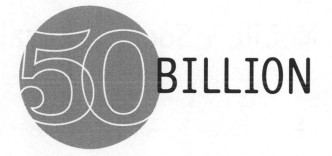

50 BILLION

Fast Casual Segment predicted to reach 50 billion in sales by 2017

46%

of consumers are now using mobile devices to access information on restaurants

Mobile + Social + Local

 Fooding